MW01257454

Faking It

Victorian Documentary Novels

Faking It

Victorian Documentary Novels

ELLEN STOCKSTILL

CLEMSON
UNIVERSITY
PRESS

First Edition, 2023

ISBN: 978-1-63804-079-8 (print)
eISBN:978-1-63804-080-4 (e-book)

Published by Clemson University Press
in association with Liverpool University Press

For information about Clemson University Press,
please visit our website at www.clemson.edu/press.

Library of Congress Cataloging-in-Publication Data
CIP Data available on request

Typeset in Minion Pro by Carnegie Book Production.
Printed and bound by CPI Group (UK) Ltd, Croydon CR0 4YY.

To all those who show us the wonders of form and
who shine gloriously in the constraints.

Contents

Figures

Acknowledgments

I never would have embarked upon or completed this project without the support of many generous and smart people. Carol Senf and Sarah Higinbotham both offered encouragement and wise counsel at the project's early stages, and Sarah's enthusiasm in particular helped buoy my confidence at low moments in the writing process. She read or listened to multiple sections of the manuscript and always offered constructive feedback and immensely generous support. Nicole Lobdell provided critical insights on Chapter 3 that helped me think through how to re-envision the section, and, as always, she was generous with her time and friendship. LeeAnne Richardson provided compassionate, wise counsel when I hit bottom in the publishing process, and I'll always be grateful for her clear guidance on how to move forward. My anonymous peer reviewers helped me refine and expand this project in key ways while also encouraging me to recognize and clearly articulate the import of my ideas. You know who you are. Thank you. Jeffrey Beck in the School of Humanities at Penn State Harrisburg was a steadfast supporter during this years-long writing and publication process, and I appreciate the knowledgeable staff, librarians, and archivists of Penn State Harrisburg, the Harry Ransom Center, Duke University, the University of Illinois, the University of California, and Archive.org for helping me access and use rare materials. I continue to be grateful for the year I spent teaching at Georgia Tech where I was first introduced to the concept of affordances, which has turned out to shape so much of my teaching and research. John Morgenstern, Alison Mero, and their team at Clemson provided smart, swift guidance as I finalized the manuscript and we collaborated on issues of design. Jody Silliker and Paul Volmer generously gave me space to work in their home when I needed writing retreats early in 2020, complete with food, fast internet, and compassionate understanding of my need for quiet space. Every time I worked at their house, I was able to pull off some sort of writing breakthrough, and I could not have completed this project without those precious bursts of productivity.

While working on this book I had a second child, struggled with writing anxiety, juggled the work–life challenges of the Covid-19 pandemic, and was often plagued by the thought that I just wouldn't have time to work. I am incredibly grateful to my family, friends, and colleagues who continued to offer encouragement while I struggled to find the time and mental space to complete this book. The love and support of my family fills me with more joy than I ever thought possible. The words "thank you" aren't enough, Drew, Lydia Grace, and River. I love you.

Introduction

Fiction, while the feigner of it knows that he is feigning,
partakes, more than we suspect, of the nature of *lying*.

Thomas Carlyle

If fiction writers are liars, in Thomas Carlyle's view, do some lie more
than others? For instance, what if they present themselves as *editors*
of historical fact rather than what they really are: weavers of narrative
fiction? Are these supposed editors, like Currer Bell of *Jane Eyre* (1847),
presenting their work differently than George Eliot, whose narrator in
the realist novel *Adam Bede* (1859) claims the book is a "faithful representing of commonplace things," and describes themselves like one "in the
witness-box narrating my experience on oath"?[1] Does this make Charlotte
Brontë's decision to present her(him)self as an editor of an autobiography
a significantly different artistic choice (and a disingenuous one) than Eliot
who openly acknowledges her work is fiction but defends its merits based
on its verisimilitude? (See Figures 1.1 and 1.2.) In other words, does a
novel *pretending to be history* function differently than a novel *claiming to
be realistic*? And if it does, how so and to what benefit?

This book seeks to answer those questions by closely examining
Victorian novels that present themselves as non-fiction works. These

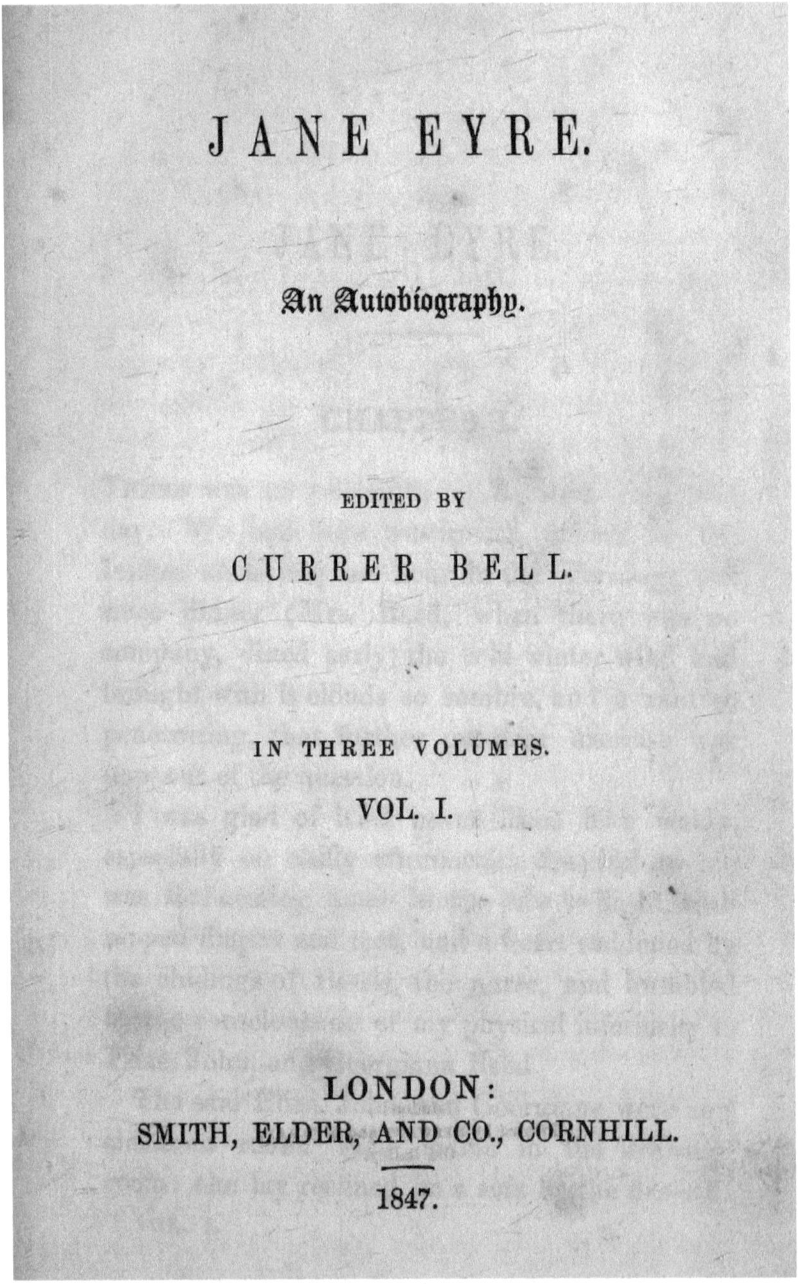

JANE EYRE.

An Autobiography.

EDITED BY

CURRER BELL.

IN THREE VOLUMES.

VOL. I.

LONDON:
SMITH, ELDER, AND CO., CORNHILL.

1847.

Figure 1.1: Charlotte Brontë, *Jane Eyre: An Autobiography*, 1847. David M. Rubenstein Rare Book & Manuscript Library, Duke University

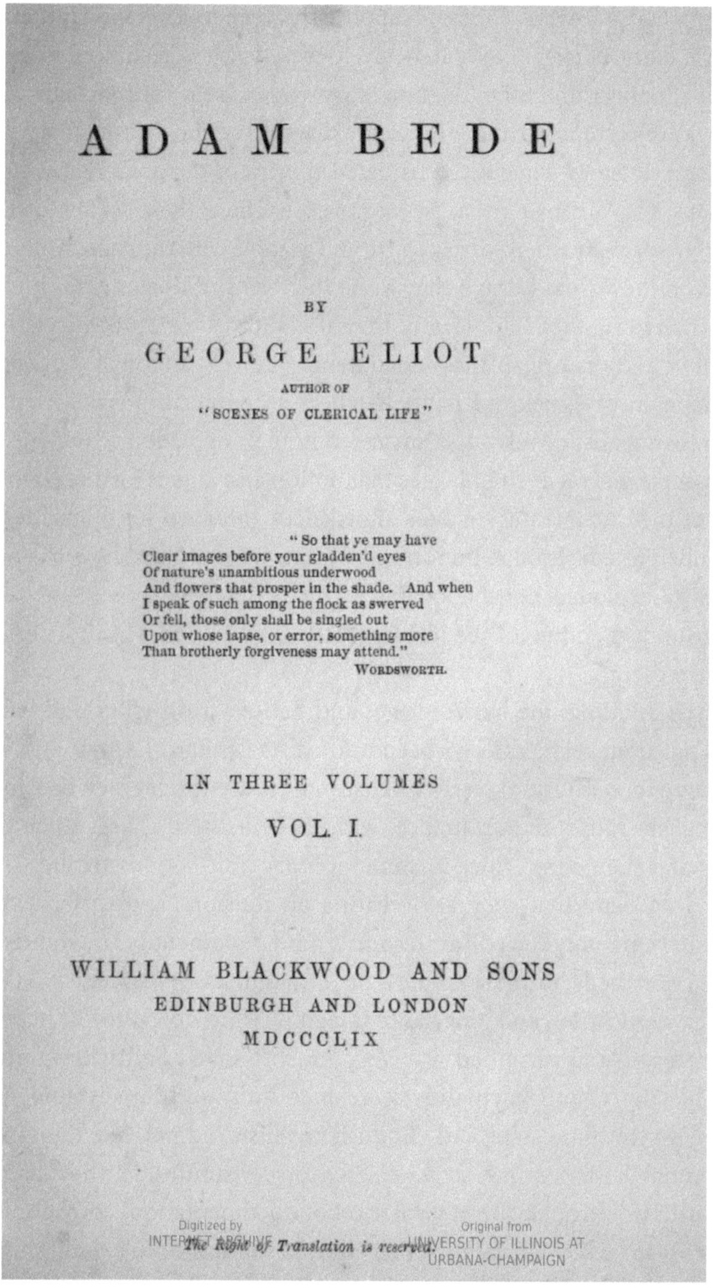

ADAM BEDE

BY

GEORGE ELIOT

AUTHOR OF

"SCENES OF CLERICAL LIFE"

"So that ye may have
Clear images before your gladden'd eyes
Of nature's unambitious underwood
And flowers that prosper in the shade. And when
I speak of such among the flock as swerved
Or fell, those only shall be singled out
Upon whose lapse, or error, something more
Than brotherly forgiveness may attend."
WORDSWORTH.

IN THREE VOLUMES

VOL. I.

WILLIAM BLACKWOOD AND SONS

EDINBURGH AND LONDON

MDCCCLIX

The Right of Translation is reserved.

Figure 1.2: George Eliot, *Adam Bede*, 1859. Rare Book & Manuscript Library, University of Illinois at Urbana-Champaign documentary novels contain supposedly authentic transcriptions of letters, diary entries, memoirs, travelogues, witness testimonies, newspaper clippings, and other documentary evidence that purportedly verify a narrative's claims of truth. They are fake works of non-fiction. In a period of literary history generally considered the era of the great realist novel, perhaps it is surprising that many novelists chose these forms for their work—especially when we recognize and grapple with the constraints they place on the writer. I argue that while the forms of documentary novels constrain the author significantly, they also afford a variety of effects, both aesthetic and rhetorical. These documentary novels, although well known and in many cases beloved, have often been seen by critics as of a lower art form than realist novels—less advanced in their depiction of real life and real people. *Faking It* complicates that notion and argues for a reexamination of the documentary novel's affordances and even flexibility, despite the inherent constraints. Importantly, when we recognize how Victorian novelists exploited non-fiction forms for fictional purposes, we gain a better understanding of the history of the English novel from its origins to the present.

The dividing line between fact and fiction, truth-teller and liar, in the English novel has always been murky. As Lennard J. Davis argues in *Factual Fictions* (1983), early English novels are the literary cousins of journalism rather than romance, with their insistent claims of authenticity and their similarities to contemporary non-fiction writing. These "novelists deny that they are creating an illusion" and instead claim "that they are only the editor to some found document."[2] The eighteenth century birthed "both the modern novel and modern journalism," Doug Underwood writes, and "one has to imagine a time when the line between the real and the imagined was very much blurred and when notions of 'objectivity' and 'factuality' were in a fluid and largely undefined state."[3] In this fluid state, early English novelists did not, like Eliot in the mid-nineteenth century, strive chiefly for verisimilitude; they claimed "historicity" through the presentation of documentation, corroborating evidence, or editorial claim, which allowed the author to exploit the line between "the real and the possibly real."[4] A novel written in the style of a travel narrative, for example, utilizes established conventions and reader expectations to present an imaginary work that, because of its "real-life" referent, is seen either as real or, at the very least, possibly real. As Underwood claims, "the writing style, authorial voice, and literary viewpoint manifested in those early novels reflect the practices of a time when journalism often looked like what we call fiction today and fiction could look like journalism."[5]

One need look no further than the title pages of a few early English novels to observe these kinds of authenticity and historical claims, crafted illusions, and the blurred line between fact and fiction. The title page of Aphra Behn's 1688 novel states it plainly: "Oroonoko; or, The Royal Slave: *A True History.*" The title page of *Robinson Crusoe* (1719) is much more elaborate:

> The Life and Strange Surprizing Adventures of Robinson Crusoe, of York, Mariner: Who lived Eight and Twenty Years, all alone in an un-inhabited island on the Coast of America, near the Mouth of the Great River Oroonoque: Having been cast on Shore by Shipwreck, wherein all the Men perished but himself with An Account how he was at last strangely deilver'd by Pyrates. *Written by Himself.*

Lastly, there is Samuel Richardson's

> Clarissa. or, the History of a Young Lady: Comprehending The most Important Concerns of Private Life. And particularly showing, The Distresses that may attend the Misconduct Both of Parents and Children, In Relation to Marriage. *Published by the Editor of Pamela.*

(Emphases added in each title.) In *Oroonoko*, Behn admits to writing the book—she does not cast herself as a mere editor—but she claims to be an "eyewitness" to many of the narrated events, and when not an eyewitness, she claims Oroonoko himself provided "whole transactions," which the reader can then trust with "there being enough of reality to support it, and to render it diverting, without the addition of invention."[6] Even Behn's opening words in *Oroonoko*, "I do not pretend ... " instill in the reader an expectation that what follows is a true representation of a *real* life.

In *Robinson Crusoe*, Defoe relies upon conventions of non-fiction writing in crafting his novel of self-reliance and survival, and, unlike Behn, he does not cast himself as a participant. Rather, he is the conveyer of these "Surprizing Adventures," written by Crusoe "himself." "Defoe," the feigner, from Carlyle's perspective,

> had no direct experience with plantations, South American coastal peoples, oceanic voyages, the slave trade, or a colonial economy. What he "knew" came through the play of his imagination on information from travel narratives, trade, geographies, etc. The actualism of his novel functions as an effective mode of deception.[7]

And Defoe's deception is twofold. As Davis writes in *Factual Fictions*, novelists like Defoe "are not merely liars by virtue of the fact that they make up stories; they are liars twice over since they deny that they have done so."[8] Bertil Romberg describes these actions as "verifying" and "detaching": "the author verifies by his own name that the stories entrusted to him, orally or in writing, are authentic, and at the same time he thereby detaches himself from authorship."[9] These denials result in "shift[ing] the focus of narrative to the being of the protagonist, to the authenticity of the document, to the verisimilar human life itself."[10] In other words, Defoe's stepping back focuses reader attention on Crusoe and *his* written document and *his* experiences rather than the skill with which Defoe has created them. Of course, it is Defoe's extraordinary skill in descriptive writing that makes the book a masterpiece. Virginia Woolf wrote that Defoe was a "genius for fact."[11] I would revise her description, if I may with sincere respect to Woolf, to a "genius for the appearance of fact," since Defoe writes in his preface to the novel, "If ever the Story of any private Man's adventures in the World were worth making Publick, and were acceptable when Publish'd, the Editor of this Account thinks this will be so. ... The Editor believes the thing to be a just History of Fact; neither is there any Appearance of Fiction in it."[12] Therein lies Defoe's masterful trick—a novel without the appearance of fiction—and it's one that many others have attempted to reproduce.[13]

Twenty-nine years later, in *Clarissa* (1748), Richardson falsely presents himself as an editor and even describes critical editorial decisions in the novel's preface, highlighting different advice he has received regarding how the volume of letters could be trimmed down to enhance the narrative. He writes, "One gentleman ... advised [me] to give a narrative turn to the letters, and to publish only what concerned the principal heroine—striking off the collateral incidents and all that related to the second characters."[14] As Richardson defends his editorial decision to include "the lives, characters, and catastrophes of several others, either principally or incidentally concerned in the story," he gives readers a sense of reality not through complete disavowal but through Richardson's supposed care and thoughtful treatment of these raw materials.[15] Unlike Defoe, who wholly distances himself from Crusoe's narrative, Richardson gives readers a supposed window into the work of an editor, describing some of the letter collection's unique qualities and the risks associated with taking a number of different steps to trim down its length. Richardson's preface to *Clarissa* communicates to his readers that he has worked carefully to consider the value of all of the story's details.

Documentary novels like those of Behn, Defoe, and Richardson dominated the British literary marketplace in the genre's early years. Conventional wisdom suggests that these seventeenth- and eighteenth-century novels were significant contributions in the history of the novel, but that they were essentially developmental—that they were a starting point for what got perfected later. The introduction to *The Cambridge Companion to the Eighteenth-Century Novel* (1996) claims just that: "Eighteenth-century 'novels' such as we now read and study represent part of the 'prehistory' of novelistic development; they constitute the early and truly formative phase of the novel as a genre of prose fiction."[16] John Richetti's description of these novels as "prehistoric" and "formative" echoes claims by many literary critics and book historians who argue that, following the ascendency of the epistolary novel in the eighteenth century, writers in the nineteenth rejected the form because of its limitations, and instead traded historicity for verisimilitude.

Scholars typically pinpoint this turn in the work of Jane Austen, master innovator of narrative style. Not only did Austen change the course of the British novel by her skillful use of free indirect style, but she also documented how she discovered the limitations of the epistolary form and then abandoned it. Joe Bray describes Austen's important role in the demise of epistolary fiction:

Though it is indisputable that many early novels were in letters, the epistolary novel has too often been treated as an isolated, digressive episode in the history of the novel as a whole, limited to the 120 years from Roger L'Estrange's first translation of *Les Lettres Portugaises* in 1678 to Jane Austen's decision in late 1797 or early 1798 to transform the probably epistolary "Elinor and Marianne" into the third-person narrative of *Sense and Sensibility*. It is often seen as an exclusively late seventeenth- and eighteenth-century phenomenon; an early, experimental form which faded away once the third-person novel began to realise its potential in the hands of novelists such as Austen and George Eliot. English Showalter's view is typical: "the epistolary novel, despite the prestige of Richardson and Rousseau, was obviously a technical dead end."[17]

Epistolary novels do indeed have significant limitations. Ian Watt, in his landmark *The Rise of the Novel: Studies in Defoe, Richardson, and Fielding* (1957), identifies some of these, including the "implausibility" that someone is sitting down to write this much material in letters on a regular basis; the repetitive nature of the form in its salutations, valedictions, and content; and the way the letters include a mass of irrelevant details to the novel's plot in order for them to seem realistic.[18] Austen's novels, from Watt's perspective, solve these issues as she is able to successfully present "authenticity without diffuseness or trickery, wisdom of social comment without a garrulous essayist, and a sense of the social order which is not achieved at the expense of the individuality and autonomy of the characters."[19] In other words, Austen's work is remarkable because her novels are not implausible in their telling, not repetitive, and do not contain a mass of irrelevant details to the novel's plot in order for them to seem realistic. Mary A. Favret writes, "With the publication of *Sense and Sensibility* in 1811, [Austen] announced her victory over the constraints of the letter," as her prose sparkles with authenticity without a need for corroborating documentary evidence.[20]

Faking It does not argue against Austen's accomplishments but rather adds further context to our understanding of narrative techniques after Austen. Austen certainly altered our sense of what was possible in narrative, and the epistolary novel never regained its preeminence, but that does not mean this type of book became extinct, that one style wholly replaced another. And yet, nearly every literature handbook, dictionary, companion, and encyclopedia implies just that, saying approximately the same thing: "After 1800 the [epistolary] form fell into almost complete disuse."[21] To claim that the epistolary novel was replaced by the realism of Jane Austen and George Eliot, among others, ignores the broader context of the epistolary novel: novels that claim to be documentary texts. When we think about the epistolary as part of this broader genre of fiction, we see that authors did not wholly abandon the kinds of framing strategies employed by writers like Behn, Defoe, and Richardson in the novel's early years. During the Victorian period, *many writers* continued to craft novels that pretend to be non-fiction—novels that, like epistolary ones, try to present themselves as historical documents such as travel narratives, case-books, autobiographies, and diaries, continuing to innovate the form, building upon and borrowing from earlier successful practitioners. These fake memoirs, diaries, correspondence, and casebooks are all significantly constrained by their documentary form—that is, the authors are limited by the type of document(s) they choose to carry their narrative. Unlike *free* indirect discourse, the narration of documentary novels is often (although not always) confined to the first person and regularly features markings of genuine non-fiction writing: diary entries are dated, letters have a defined audience, and witness testimonies identify their authors. Because the limitations seem overt and cumbersome, many critics have ignored this rich tradition of writing in the English canon or at least have preferred elevating novels with omniscient third-person narrators and subtle, effective use of focalization. The epistolary novel's decline in popularity, which has informed scholarship, claiming that early English novels were prehistoric and formative, has misled scholars into thinking that Victorian innovations and achievements in fiction lie exclusively in realism. Wayne C. Booth noted this scholarly tendency as far back as 1961 in *The Rhetoric of Fiction*, calling it a "fashionable assumption that all good fiction tries for the same kind of vivid illusion in the same way."[22] This assumption continues to be fashionable, but when we examine the breadth and origi-nality of Victorian documentary novels, we must acknowledge that our previous conception of the novel's history has been flawed because these novels were not outliers or historical anomalies; these novels were written by some of the most beloved writers of the age, including the Brontës, Charles Dickens, William Makepeace Thackeray, Wilkie Collins, Robert Louis Stevenson, and Bram Stoker.

Accordingly, this book establishes a family tree of documentary novels in order to demonstrate the interconnectedness of a variety of Victorian works. Previous histories of the novel have taken a linear and Whiggish approach, emphasizing key moments of innovation and projecting a progressive view of the novel's development (i.e., that over the course of time authors have discovered better ways of narrating human experience). Rather than a timeline, *Faking It* presents a tree, emphasizing related forms that make up the broader cultural context of the documentary novel. George Levine, in *How to Read the Victorian Novel* (2007), takes a similar approach, writing that Victorian novels have "family resemblances" that are useful in helping us define what these books share in common.[23] Although he uses the metaphor to help connect seemingly disparate texts under the umbrella of the "Victorian novel," I use it here to make sensible groupings of documentary novels, spotlighting specific subgenres that intentionally mime non-fiction documents, including letters, diaries and autobiographies, travel narratives, and casebooks. While I could arrange these books by tradition (e.g., gothic novels, domestic fiction, imperial novels, etc.), doing so would lose my desired emphasis on the formal constraints of documents used as narrative tools. I do not mean to suggest that these novels exist outside of those traditions and their preoccupations, but I do intend to illuminate, first and foremost, the types of documents novelists choose to narrate their novels in order to better understand this choice and its attending ramifications. As Booth claims, "To write one kind of book is always to some extent a repudiation of other kinds."[24] Consequently, the central questions animating each chapter of *Faking It* are: "Why did the author choose to write the book in this form and what are the impacts of that decision? What is the benefit or significance of faking it?"

The metaphor of a family tree also emphasizes the legacy of early English novels. While timeline, linear models of literary history tend to underscore major shifts or breaks with tradition, a family tree tracks meaningful connections between the past and present. Victorian documentary novels connect to the earliest novels in the English language like *Oroonoko* and *Robinson Crusoe*, and they also connect to twentieth- and twenty-first-century novels utilizing documentary forms. Alexandra Valint makes a similar claim in *Narrative Bonds: Multiple Narrators in the Victorian Novel* (2021), noting that twentieth-century multi-narrator novels by writers like William Faulkner and Virginia Woolf "have long been described as 'experimental.'" "The traditional narrative of literary history," she continues, "presents modernism as a radical break with the conventional Victorian period, particularly with regards to form. Considering the multiperspectival structure as a through line *links rather than divides* these novels—they are not just silos of experimentalism" (emphasis added).[25] Similarly, my family tree model of literary history places experimentation in context, noting points of connection as well as deviation, and the tree's status as a living document opens the possibility that this genealogy will be amended as other researchers draw connections between documentary novels of the Victorian period and those in the following centuries—something I will discuss explicitly in the conclusion of this book.

A tree diagram emphasizes legacy while also encouraging us to consider the relationships between literary genres and forms. Narratologists have regularly identified Austen as the key innovator in nineteenth-century fiction, and rightfully so, suggesting a seismic shift in her wake, but documentary and realist novels are not diametrically opposed, completely unlinked modes of writing.[26] Booth and Lilian R. Furst make this clear in *The Rhetoric of Fiction* and *All is True: The Claims and Strategies of Realist Fiction* (1995) respectively. Booth writes, "Much of our scholarly and critical work of the highest seriousness has, in fact, employed this same dialectical opposition between artful showing and inartistic, merely rhetorical, telling."[27] He emphasizes that realist fiction should not be considered more natural than the alternatives: "Whatever verisimilitude a work may have always operates within a larger artifice; each work that succeeds is natural—and artificial—in its own way."[28] Furst extends Booth's argument and notes how realist novelists "were remarkably successful" in "conceal[ing] the literariness of their practices. In a sense, therefore, the realist novel can be seen as a prodigious cover-up."[29] In other words, Austen's skillful narration and strategic use of free indirect discourse work to make her guiding hand invisible, but her hand is there nonetheless. "Realism" like this, James Wood writes, "offers the appearance of reality but is in fact utterly fake—what Barthes calls 'the referential illusion.'"[30] Furst, Booth, and Wood thus recognize that the novelist is always constructing an illusion and making decisions about how to write and what to emphasize. True, realist fiction tends to minimize readers' awareness of its rhetoric, but the great realists of the nineteenth century are just as invested in illusion as the writers of documentary fiction. In short, they are all faking it. As Furst writes, "Although some fictions choose constantly to underscore their own fictionality ... and some assume the contrary posture by accentuating verisimilitude (as does the realist novel), all of them partake of both fictionality and verisimilitude, the difference lying only in proportion and emphasis."[31] We must recognize then the absurdity or the inadequacy, at least, of automatically positioning realism as the norm from which all other modes of fiction writing deviate.[32] It makes perfect sense to distinguish between novels that accentuate verisimilitude and those that underscore their fictionality (in Booth's terms, those that *show* from those that *tell*), but we err if we then make a value judgment based on that difference and if we overemphasize one genre's capacity to illustrate complex and compelling human experiences.

This means we can take documentary novels seriously as works of art. The novels I discuss here do not cover up their narrational strategies (in many instances they are even labeled and discussed for the reader). They tend to draw attention to themselves as constructed texts, and many critics over the years have judged their paratextual elements, framing devices, and direct addresses to the reader as akin to cheap tricks or bothersome window dressing. The most skilled novelists, the thinking goes, make their presence invisible. *Faking It* interrogates that long-held claim and considers thoroughly the novelist's decision to embrace the constraints and conventions of the documentary form. For, despite the tendency to view documentary novels as merely residual, holdovers from an earlier era of fiction writing, or extinct from the world of literary excellence, this type of fiction not only persists, but it has a rich history and legacy. "The attraction of this form of writing," Underwood notes, "has been strong throughout history."[33] Examining these novels on their own terms, then, attuned to their affordances, *Faking It* highlights the achievements of

Victorian writers who worked creatively within the constraints of the documentary form and argues that their achievements reveal, at least in part, why novelists continue to write documentary fiction today.

Before building out the dimensions of this family tree, a few words about the term "documentary novel," which I follow Barbara Foley and Troy J. Bassett in using. Scholars have given novels presented as non-fiction a number of different names, including "nonfiction novel," "fictive realism," "factual fiction," "news/novels discourse," "fiction of authentic documents," "formal realism," "manuscript fiction," and the "eyewitness form."[34] Each of these terms has its advantages and in general gets the point across. "Documentary novel," however, has some distinct advantages that help distinguish this genre from others popular during the Victorian period. First and foremost, it emphasizes the presence of documentation, corroborating material evidence. As Bassett describes it, documentary novels are those "partially or completely composed of documents such as court reports, diaries, journals, letters, newspaper articles, or telegrams."[35] Some make use of one type of document (like Laurence Housman in *An Englishwoman's Love-Letters*), while others mix types together (like Bram Stoker in *Dracula*). While Foley discusses nineteenth-century novels only briefly in *Telling the Truth: The Theory and Practice of Documentary Fiction* (1986), *Faking It* explores Victorian novels that make a "claim to empirical validation" through the author's crafting of artificial "authentic" documents.[36]

While many English novels include references to and excerpts from letters, telegrams, or other documents, this book focuses on novels that use documents to carry the narrative entirely. In these novels, the document or collection of documents *is* the novel and as such the material condition of the text contributes significantly to its meaning. *Faking It* does not include Victorian novels that partially use documents, for two reasons. First, novels that feature a small number of letters or other documents have been covered sufficiently elsewhere.[37] Second, one of my primary interests in this book is the matter of creativity within constraints. It is one thing to include Darcy's letter to Elizabeth in *Pride and Prejudice* explaining his past behavior. It is quite another to narrate the novel entirely through dialogic correspondence. Despite the inherent limitations of writing a documentary novel, however, novelists have continued to write them.

My exploration of these Victorian novels narrated entirely through documents is thus a probe into that choice and the ways writers work creatively and strategically within such significant constraints.

While the terms "nonfiction novel," "factual fiction," and "eyewitness form" are quite similar and could be useful, many first-person novels could fit under those terms whether they include documentary evidence or not. A first-person *Bildungsroman*, for example, presents as a kind of presumed nonfiction in which the author has created a sense of intimacy and authenticity by having the novel narrated by the protagonist. Who is a better eyewitness than the hero himself? Documentary novels, however, differ in that they provide readers with material(s) that supposedly "prove" the veracity of the narrative. These may be corroborating letters, explanatory footnotes, archeological evidence, or editorial statements (among others). Consider, for instance, the opening of Charles Dickens's first-person *Bildungsroman*, *Great Expectations* (1860–61), in which Pip describes the provenance of his name: "My father's family name being Pirrip, and my Christian name Philip, my infant tongue could make of both names nothing longer or more explicit than Pip. So, I called myself Pip, and came to be called Pip."[38] These two sentences establish the intimacy with which Pip will tell his own life story. As Pip continues, his childlike interpretations enhance our sense that Dickens has presented us with the authentic memories of a young boy:

> As I never saw my father or my mother, and never saw any likeness of either of them (for their days were long before the days of photographs), my first fancies regarding what they were like, were unreasonably derived from their tombstones. The shape of the letters on my father's, gave me an odd idea that he was a square, stout, dark man, with curly black hair. From the character and turn of the inscription, "Also Georgiana Wife of the Above," I drew a childish conclusion that my mother was freckled and sickly.[39]

While we can marvel at Dickens's masterful construction of Pip as a realistic and empathetic narrator of this fictional autobiography, *Great Expectations* is not a documentary novel. No material evidence supports the assertion that Pip is a real boy, that his family members lie buried under the earth in that cemetery, or that he had a strange encounter with an escaped convict. Furthermore, life-writing documentary novels carry the potential to comment on the act of writing itself in a manner quite different than other first-person novels. Certainly, a first-person novel may feature an unreliable narrator, but, as I outline in Chapter 2, a life-writing documentary novel may feature an unreliable document that draws our attention to the inherent limitations of language and narrative.

The term "documentary novel" also helps distinguish this category from historical fiction, a genre that gained prominence in the nineteenth century thanks to writers like Sir Walter Scott, Charles Dickens, and William Makepeace Thackeray. In *The English Historical Novel: Walter Scott to Virginia Woolf* (1971), Avrom Fleishman writes that "novels set in the past—beyond an arbitrary number of years, say 40–60 (two generations)—are liable to be considered historical," and that in their "substance, there is an unspoken assumption that the plot must include a number of 'historical' events, particularly those in the public sphere (war, politics, economic change, etc.), mingled with and affecting the personal fortunes of the characters."[40] Unlike historical novels, documentary ones do not require an earlier setting. Indeed, many carry a sense of immediacy. In a novel of letters or diary entries, for instance, the protagonist–writer records her experiences as they occur or in their immediate aftermath. Furthermore, although documentary novels may claim to be historical records (that is, authentic reports of real people in the real world) they do not necessarily connect to historical events or figures. Anne Brontë's *The Tenant of Wildfell Hall* (1848), which I discuss in Chapter 1, claims historical reality as a text made up of letters and diary entries, but the novel focuses entirely on the relationships between characters, not on any historical event or actors of great importance. One could argue, in fact, that documentary and historical novels are inverse forms. Documentary novels deny their fictionality and claim connection with the real world through constructed material evidence, while historical novels admit their fictionality but claim connection with the real world through characters' relationships with historical people and experiences of actual events. Both are mimetic forms, but the former's mimesis lies in its mimicry of non-fiction writing and the latter's mimesis lies in its cast of characters, setting, and action. Fleishman writes,

> The presence of a realistic background for the action is a widespread characteristic of the novel, and many panoramic social novels are deep in history. The historical novel is distinguished among novels by the presence of a specific link to history: not merely a real building or a real event but a real person among the fictitious ones. When life is seen in the context of history, we have a novel; when the novel's characters live in the same world with historical persons, we have a historical novel.[41]

One might add, when the action of the novel and the thoughts of the characters are documented in letters, diaries, autobiographies, travel journals, or casebooks, we have a documentary novel.

Writers of historical fiction use a number of techniques to ground their work in reality, to convince readers of their book's historical plausibility, but documentary novels do not necessarily seek to do so. An author may choose to craft a novel as a document or collection of documents in an attempt to convey a sense of reality, but he may also write a documentary novel because of its narrative affordances. Wilkie Collins's primary drive in constructing *The Moonstone* (1868) as a series of documents, for instance, was not a desire for historical accuracy or plausibility. Collins's genius in this touchstone work of detective fiction is his use of different narrative perspectives to build suspense and to both reveal and conceal information at the same time. As I argue in Chapter 4, he essentially turns the epistolary novel's limited point of view into an asset. By giving us the perspective of only one character at a time through written testimonies, with all their biases, Collins keeps us in the dark as to the true identity of the diamond thief through much of the novel. While scholars have pointed out the ways this kind of limited perspective causes technical difficulties in an epistolary novel, intentionally limiting the reader's access to key information in a mystery like *The Moonstone* allows the writer to retain reader interest while building a labyrinth around the truth of the case.

This book argues, then, that Victorian novelists were motivated to write documentary fiction for a number of different reasons. "Faking it" does not mean that an author's only purpose in presenting fiction as fact is to trick readers into belief. Rather, the "fake" letters, diaries, travel journals, or notes might be used for a number of reasons. This is an important corrective to the misrepresentation of the novel's history in which verisimilitude replaced historicity. In this version of history, Austen ushered in a new world where novelists could more successfully convey reality than previous writers who relied upon the cumbersome presence of validating documentary evidence. But to see documentary novels as useful only in this light ignores their potential—potential that many writers in the Victorian period decided to tap. If we evaluate these books only by their ability to convey a sense of reality, we ignore how writers utilized a full range of affordances of non-fiction writing when crafting their novels. Furthermore, to do so would perpetuate the pervasive notion that realism is "the norm from which other modes ... are variants or deviants."[42]

The term "*affordance*" comes from design theory, but literary scholars, principally Caroline Levine in Victorian studies, have used it to illuminate each literary form's innate possibilities. For the purposes of this monograph, thinking about affordances helps us reshape our understanding of documentary fiction in the Victorian period. As I have already described, historians of the novel have regularly claimed that documentary novels of the seventeenth and eighteenth centuries were discovered to be too constraining for writers. These constraints can indeed be significant—whether it be the demands of crafting a compelling first-person narrative, the restrictions of parroting non-fiction documents, the challenge of creating multiple authentic voices that communicate back and forth, the temporal difficulties of supposedly on-the-spot writing, or the extreme limitations on point of view. These constraints have traditionally been seen as unsurmountable problems inherent in the documentary form that wiser and more modern writers abandoned for other narrative styles. In *Forms: Whole, Rhythm, Hierarchy, Network* (2015), Levine argues, however, that "'form' always indicates *an arrangement of elements—an ordering, patterning, or shaping*," and, as such, "*Forms constrain.*"[43] The constraints of the documentary form may be plainly apparent, but all forms constrain, and, as I will show throughout this book, many Victorian novelists display remarkable creativity as they work within the constraints of documentary fiction. Indeed, many of their books *work* because of the inherent constraints of documentary novels. As Levine writes in "Not Against Structure, but in Search of Better Structures," "Every form constrains, but it also enables—it capacitates. If an enclosed space shuts in and excludes, it also affords security and shelter, a desirable space away from noise and cold."[44]

In every chapter of this book, then, I elucidate the constraints of four subgenres of documentary novels. In doing so, I also highlight what those constraints afford. Following Levine, I recognize that "Affordances point us both to what all forms are capable of—to the range of uses each could be put to … —and also to their limits, the restrictions intrinsic to particular materials and organizing principles."[45] I also adhere to the idea that these novelists chose the documentary form with intention, sharing with James Phelan and Peter J. Rabinowitz an interest "in why the narrative text is the way it is and not some other way."[46] Each chapter that follows represents a branch on the family tree of Victorian documentary novels distinguished by the type of document the novel uses as its mode of delivery: (1) letters; (2) autobiographies, memoirs, or diaries; (3) travel narratives or journals; and (4) casebooks.

In Chapter 1, I describe the constraints and affordances of epistolary novels and consider how two novelists use the form for very different ends. Citing a letter-writing manual from 1812, I establish three traits of personal correspondence that help us understand why novelists continued to utilize the epistolary form into the nineteenth century and beyond. I first highlight Anne Brontë's use of an epistolary frame in *The Tenant of Wildfell Hall* (1848) to document the horrors of an abusive relationship and society's failure to address that abuse. While scholars have debated Brontë's chosen form and argued over Gilbert Markham's troubling decision to transcribe Helen Huntingdon's diary into a letter for a friend, I show how Brontë's choice of narrative form privileges subjectivity and intimacy and helps her emphasize the damage done by English education and marriage customs. I strategically juxtapose *The Tenant of Wildfell Hall* with a novel largely unknown today that was immensely popular when published in 1900: Laurence Housman's *An Englishwoman's Love-Letters*. Markedly different than Brontë's novel in terms of style, Housman's book was carefully marketed as a real collection of love letters and was published at a cultural moment of fascination with romantic correspondence and the boundaries between public and private. The novel contains realistic monologic letters, and the mystery surrounding the book's source material and content inspired debate on the capacities of letter writing and the ethics of publishing private correspondence. My consideration of *The Tenant of Wildfell Hall* and *Love-Letters* together underscores an underappreciated flexibility of the epistolary form and reveals how it capacitates novelists to play with or, at least, explore that slippery territory between public and private.

Chapter 2 features what I refer to as life-writing documentary novels—fake autobiographies, memoirs, and diaries. I place five Victorian novels on a spectrum, positioning them by how they utilize the affordances of the subgenre and whether they draw attention to their constructedness as texts. Considering them this way underscores that although these novels purportedly present genuine works of life writing, they differ remarkably in what they reveal about society, identity, and the capacity to narrate human life effectively. While an autobiography novel like *Jane Eyre*, for instance, enhances our belief in a stable and socialized identity, a biography novel like Thomas Carlyle's *Sartor Resartus* (1834) shows that fashioning an honest narrative about a person's life is a fool's errand. We habitually contend that Victorian life-writing novels are dominated by the master-narrative of "progress," but we ignore texts like *Sartor Resartus* and William Makepeace Thackeray's *The Memoirs of Barry Lyndon, Esq.* (1844), which instead of leading towards enlightenment, social integration, and identity cohesion, advance towards confusion, disconnect, or delusion.

Chapter 3 examines the travel and adventure writing of Robert Louis Stevenson and H. Rider Haggard. Using popular Victorian books of travel writing by Isabella Bird, Mary Seacole, Henry Morton Stanley, and Mary Kingsley, I establish this subgenre's range of affordances and consider how Stevenson and Haggard make use of them in their novels. I argue that the former does so in surprising ways despite the limitations inherent in a first-person narrative, while the latter tends to merely default to the conventional and the cliché. In a subgenre of documentary novels with firmly established norms—so established we might even think of them as actively destructive to creative work—I invite readers to marvel at Stevenson's achievements in *Treasure Island* (1883) but also to consider how this form of documentary fiction, and the way it has been copied and recopied, has repeatedly privileged a Western gaze.

My final chapter covers novels regarded as some of the most compelling examples of Victorian documentary fiction: the casebook novels of Wilkie Collins, Charles Warren Adams, and Bram Stoker. I use the term "*casebook*" in keeping with books going back to the seventeenth and eighteenth centuries kept as legal records and as doctors' notebooks. These casebooks were a highly flexible and composite form made up of various materials and types of writing. Similarly, *The Woman in White* (1859–60), *The Moonstone* (1868), *The Notting Hill Mystery* (1863), and *Dracula* (1897) all combine different kinds of texts, and the authors make strategic use of the documentary form's tendency to significantly limit point of view. I argue that mystery, sensation, and horror fiction benefit markedly from the limitations inherent in this form because they enhance the reader's experience of suspense and constrain their access to the truth of the case. I also suggest that these casebook novels reveal an almost postmodern distrust of language and experiential knowledge to accurately capture certain experiences. These casebook novels repeatedly show, in fact, the difficulty of achieving meaningful communication or closure when faced with horrifying acts of greed, violence, and manipulation.

I conclude by looking at this rich tradition beyond the nineteenth century, inviting scholars to extend the family tree of Victorian documentary novels I have established here. I offer an analysis of Kazuo Ishiguro's *The Remains of the Day* (1989), a novel that explodes this notion that documentary novels lack the psychological depth and complex characterizations of novels featuring omniscient third-person narrators and free indirect discourse. In fact, the novel's complex portrait of an aging butler is made possible by its constrained documentary form. As Monika Gehlawat writes, "Formalism is the key to *The Remains of the Day* ... [It] is constructed as a kind of Russian nesting doll of creative workmanship."[47] This kind of workmanship, I argue, has important pedagogical and political implications because documentary novels, from the beginning of the genre's history to the present day, illustrate the human capacity to push against seemingly intractable constraints.

No other book-length study has examined this family of novels in concert with each other, and the advantages of doing so include expanding our understanding of narrative innovations in the nineteenth century, complicating our notion of realism and conveyed "reality" in a fictional work, emphasizing Mikhail Bakhtin's notion that the novel "parodies other genres," and helping us recognize how novels of the twentieth and twenty-first centuries continue to extend this family tree.[48]

CHAPTER ONE

Epistolary Novels

A Persisting Subgenre

This chapter acknowledges that the epistolary novel never regained its footing as the preeminent mode of fiction writing in British culture after 1800, but it also contends that the form remained useful for writers into and beyond the Victorian period because of its inherent narrative qualities.[1] Claiming so pushes back against English Showalter's notion of the epistolary novel as "obviously a technical dead end."[2] *Faking It* places the epistolary novel in the broader context of documentary fiction in order to show how writers successfully used not only letters but a variety of document types as their narrative vehicles in the Victorian period. Here I enumerate the technical constraints of the epistolary subgenre and endeavor to show the creative ways skilled authors worked within those constraints and tapped into the form's narrative potential. This chapter, in conjunction with those that follow, demonstrates the ways form shapes meaning; in the case of documentary novels, the type of document the author chooses as a narrative vehicle profoundly impacts our understanding of it. My analysis of epistolary novels underscores that the narrative vehicle of the letter is more versatile than often noted and is linked intimately to the real, social world— long considered the prominent domain of the realist novel.

In the Introduction I described the various narrative difficulties inherent in the epistolary form and highlighted Jane Austen's pivotal role in breaking out of the epistolary's constraints. These limitations include the epistolary novel's supposed implausibility, repetitive nature, limited perspective, and inclusion of irrelevant details, making up "the sometimes achingly artificial nature of its narrative techniques when seen alongside the third-person novel."[3] Despite these well-documented drawbacks, these limitations do not make epistolary novels a failed or extinct form. Just because the epistolary novel's popularity with writers and readers waned in the nineteenth century does not mean that the form disappeared or that authors wholly abandoned its features. As Kathleeen Martha Ward writes,

> All through the nineteenth century, epistolary fiction continued to appear—some of it very good, some of it quite dreadfully bad. Dozens of epistolary novels were written in Britain between 1800 and 1900. True, novelists during the nineteenth century no longer automatically chose to write novels in the form of letters, but they did turn frequently to letter fiction for special purposes, making use of its advantages and confronting its drawbacks.[4]

Showalter's claim that the epistolary novel is a dead end assumes all writers are trying to get to the same destination. In the case of English literary history, many scholars have named that destination free indirect discourse, the nineteenth-century's supreme literary accomplishment.[5] George Levine helpfully corrects this one-sided view: "There are many variations in the Victorian pursuit of the right sort of narrator, the right way to represent the experience to be narrated."[6] *Faking It* highlights those novels in which the author represents the experience to be narrated through a certain type or types of documents, and this chapter shows how letters serve as "the right way" for these particular literary texts.

I focus on two epistolary novels that are different than each other in nearly every measurable way: the authors' purpose in writing them, their critical reception, and their lasting value. Additionally, and more to the purposes of this book, the novels use the epistolary form to achieve different ends. Anne Brontë's *The Tenant of Wildfell Hall* (1848) exposes the horrors of an abusive marriage in letters and transcribed diary entries, documents associated with privacy, personal experience and reflection, and social relationships. Brontë does so in a format that does not mimic actual correspondence; she does not concern herself with making the letters of *The Tenant of Wildfell Hall* seem real. Rather, she seeks to faithfully document men's behavior in a form that privileges individual experience. Laurence Housman's *An Englishwoman's Love-Letters* (1900), on the other hand, takes the opposite tactic, closely mimicking letter-writing conventions not to address a societal problem like Brontë but to take advantage of a cultural moment in which people were debating the boundary between public and private. The stark differences between these two novels reveal a flexibility in the epistolary mode which has been largely ignored as critics have mostly focused on the limitations inherent in epistolary writing without considering its assets or versatility.

Thomas Cooke's "Preface" to *The Universal Letter-Writer* (1775) offers guidance in understanding the assets of the epistolary form. Cooke's book is one of many letter-writing manuals republished during the nineteenth century and part of a tradition going back to the Elizabethan era.[7] His preface to this "how-to" manual underscores the "great utility of epistolary writing"—a kind of "art replete with such advantages" that it "is needless to insist upon" how important it is to know how to write letters. Although he claims that it is "needless" to explain the value of knowledge in this field, he describes the letter's distinct advantages:

> Had letters been known at the beginning of the world, Epistolary Writing would have been as old as love and friendship; for, as soon as they began to flourish, the verbal messenger was dropt, the language of the heart was committed to characters that faithfully preserved it, secrecy was maintained, and social intercourse rendered more free and agreeable.[8]

Cooke writes that letters replaced the "verbal messenger" as a preferred communication tool for three reasons: letters are *faithful*, *secret*, and *social*. Letters faithfully preserve "the language of the heart"; they are secret as private, sealed correspondence; and they are social in their ability to connect individuals and sustain relationships. These benefits reward not just one group of people, but, as Cooke claims, "letters are the life of trade, the fuel of love, the pleasure of friendship, the food of the politician, and the entertainment of the curious."[9] In my examination of Victorian epistolary novels, I use Cooke's language of the faithful, secret, and social letter to inform my analysis as I emphasize how writers take advantage of these qualities to create fake correspondence.[10] I thus draw attention to the possibilities of epistolary fiction to show that this subgenre of documentary novels, this branch of the family tree, is not a dead end, but a fruitful bough with a considerable number of cultural descendants stretching into the twenty-first century.[11]

The Tenant of *Wildfell Hall*

The Tenant of Wildfell Hall serves as a compelling site for this kind of investigation because readers and critics have not agreed about the book's value or the purpose of Brontë's use of letters. A close study of the novel and Brontë's narrative technique, including its merits and defects, can reveal what Caroline Levine calls the "limited range of potentialities" of epistolary fiction.[12] In the following pages, I detail how *The Tenant of Wildfell Hall*'s epistolary frame has frustrated readers, and the ways Brontë's text conforms to and diverges from previous models of epistolary fiction. In doing so, I acknowledge the significant constraints of this kind of documentary writing, but I also underscore how Brontë exploits some of those constraints and delivers a compelling narrative about a bright young woman who becomes trapped in a marriage characterized by disturbing scenes of intimidation, inebriation, abandonment, and dishonesty. Specifically, I respond to criticism that the epistolary frame of the novel weakens the text because of the letters' implausibility and argue that Brontë did not intend to create realistic documents to narrate her novel but to faithfully represent individual experiences through a medium associated with privacy and social connection. Her experiment in *The Tenant of Wildfell Hall* reveals that epistolary framing techniques, often seen as too synthetic or overly manufactured, do not automatically connote detachment from the real. After all, as discussed in the Introduction, a realist novel is as manufactured as any epistolary one.

The frame of the novel reveals that Gilbert Markham is writing to his brother-in-law Jack Halford in penance for having declined on an earlier occasion to offer a "return of confidence" through the sharing of a personal story.[13] Halford, in an act of trust and friendship, one imagines, had shared with Gilbert a story from his own life, only to be met with silence. Wounded by this refusal to respond in kind, Halford's letters to Gilbert "have, ever since, been distinguished by a certain dignified, semi-melancholy stiffness and reserve."[14] Now, "alone in [his] library," having perused "certain musty old letters and papers, and musing on past times," Gilbert tells Halford that he is "now in a very proper frame of mind" to tell "an old world story."[15] He thus embarks on his effort to appease his friend and relative by providing "a tale of many chapters" that is "a full and faithful account of certain circumstances connected with the most important events of [his] life."[16] He offers the "first instalment" of this tale as "coin" to pay his "debt" to Halford and pledges that he will share the rest if Halford is pleased with this initial payment and the promise of more to come.[17]

While frame narratives usually provide readers a way into the text, albeit sometimes an artificial one, what strikes many as ill-fitting about Brontë's epistolary frame in *The Tenant of Wildfell Hall* is its improbability. Does this kind of minor slip in a friendship demand such a protracted response? As Jan B. Gordon notes, the novel "quickly calls attention to itself as the longest single-narrative, enclosing epistolary novel of the nineteenth century. Beginning 'dear Halford,' it concludes four hundred and fifty pages later with a 'Til then, farewell, Gilbert Markham.'"[18] Has Gilbert really transcribed his and Helen's experiences across hundreds of pages to send by post to his brother-in-law in order to address a faux pas committed at their last meeting? Does Brontë expect her readers to consider the premise of these letters, their composition, and sending realistic, likely, or even possible?[19] Ward writes, "Letters that run into the hundreds of pages strain the limits of even the most generous definition of the epistolary form, and critics have been less than generous" to books that do so, including *The Tenant of Wildfell Hall*.[20]

While readers have complained of *The Tenant of Wildfell Hall*'s letters as implausible, Brontë did not craft an epistolary novel designed to fool readers into thinking that the text's pages are genuine correspondence. If she had, one presumes that Gilbert's letters would be much shorter and would contain significantly less dialogue and detail about people and events from years past. Rather, Brontë uses letters as her narrative vehicle for their ability to accentuate individual experience, promote private reflection, and embody social critique. In *The Universal Letter-Writer*, Cooke articulates that letters are faithful, secret, and social. The faithfulness of *The Tenant of Wildfell Hall*'s letters comes not in their mimicry of actual correspondence but in their candid conveyance of difficult truths—truths which have maximum impact when communicated by a first-person narrator. The fact that Helen reports on her own experiences in her diary lends legitimacy to them since she documents in real time her troubled relationship with her husband in a form that is secret and short-sighted. In turn, Gilbert's reading of, learning from, and sharing of her diary (all communicated through letters) demonstrate his trust of the material and the evidence of its transformative power. Diaries and letters are the repositories of human experience; when those experiences are troubling, the personal recording of them to paper suggests the plausibility of their occurrence even without the postmark on the envelope or the crease in the page. The letters' verisimilitude in the case of *The Tenant of Wildfell Hall* derives from their intimacy with the writer and their inclusion of graphic details not their correlation with what real letters actually look like. This distinguishes *The Tenant of Wildfell Hall* from other Victorian epistolary novels like Laurence Housman's *An Englishwoman's Love-Letters*, whose physical construction as a published book was designed with "a cream vellum jacket with gold embossing on the spine and two green silk ties to heighten its impression of intimacy" and whose correspondence aligns more closely with letter-writing conventions.[21] Housman's book, anonymously published and presented in diary-like packaging, played up the possibility that readers would, as indeed they did, consider the included letters genuine. Brontë's approach to faithfulness differs significantly, but it also connects *The Tenant of Wildfell Hall* to many epistolary novels that came before it that also are implausible in their length but realistic in their documentation of private thoughts and life, with probably the best example being Richardson's *Clarissa*, "By far the longest novel in the English canon."[22]

Brontë's decision to narrate the shocking behavior of men in diary entries that are then transcribed into Gilbert's letters to Halford indicates her desire to select a narrative style that accentuates human subjectivity as well as legitimates the experiences narrated therein. *The Tenant of Wildfell Hall* grants readers only Helen's perspective on her marriage and then Gilbert's reaction to that perspective. In this way, the narrative is highly subjective, subject to these two characters' interpretations of events. At the same time, however, their composing of these documents with all their horrid details offers readers the sensation of being there and witnessing real behavior. Elizabeth Hollis Berry writes, "As a means of adding veracity and dramatic force to her narrative, the epistolary framework, with its enclosed account of Helen Huntingdon's marriage (written from Helen's point of view), is psychologically effective."[23] In other words, Brontë could have written Helen's story in a less-mediated form, as some critics have suggested, but the letter format carries with it the intimation of a trusted reader with whom candid material can be shared. Furthermore, the eyewitness quality of both the diary entries and letters privileges the experience of the individual. If Brontë had written *The Tenant of Wildfell Hall* with a George Eliot-style omniscient narrator, the novel would certainly retain its gravity and pathos, but it would also implicitly suggest that someone viewing the events from the outside can understand fully what is going on. By giving Helen the platform to speak these ugly truths for herself, Brontë grants her a rare opportunity for a woman in her position to speak openly about her abuse, without interruption, correction, or amelioration by a man or some other authoritative voice. Helen's diary contains "the evidence that a married woman could not give in a court of law, since she would be femme covert or 'covered by' the body of her husband, subsumed in his identity,"[24] and Brontë's "choice of a first-person female narrator, and of the diary form, while not exactly silencing the male voice or male attitude, tips the balance of narrative power in favour of the female. Arthur and his male friends are never permitted to defend themselves."[25]

We know that Brontë wanted the book to faithfully represent real, private life even when that life contains scenes of disturbing behavior. In her "Preface to the Second Edition," she directly addresses her purpose in writing *The Tenant of Wildfell Hall* declaring,

> My object in writing the following pages, was not simply to amuse the Reader, neither was it to gratify my own taste, nor yet to ingratiate myself with the Press and the Public: I wished to tell the truth, for truth always conveys its own moral to those

who are able to receive it … Let it not be imagined, however, that I consider myself competent to reform the errors and abuses of society, but only that I would fain contribute my humble quota towards so good an aim; and if I can gain the public ear at all, I would rather whisper a few wholesome truths therein than much soft nonsense.[26]

Brontë's declaration clarifies her intention that *The Tenant of Wildfell Hall* serve a moral purpose by offering "the truth," and reveals her awareness of the key difficulties of the text and her understanding of its critics, including those who saw the novel as questionable in subject matter and construction, since the truths she conveys in the novel aren't particularly pretty to look at: the naivety of a young bride entering into a marriage with a man rumored to be a profligate; the ways a woman can become victim to marriage laws and customs that significantly disadvantage her legally, financially, and psychologically; a man's decline into alcoholism and destructive, manipulative, and controlling behavior toward his wife and child; a wife's realization of her dire situation and her society's seemingly intractable double standard; the bold actions required of a wife to leave her abusive husband; and English society's complicity in the wife's torments. Arthur, Helen's husband, not only drinks too much, but he also engages in an array of behaviors that "firmly establish a pattern of intimidation and control" in his marriage.[27] He absents himself from their home for months on end while demanding that she "write to him constantly,"[28] regularly casts himself as the victim of her emotional whims, purposefully makes her jealous for his own amusement, brings his mistress into their home as a guest, attempts to pit their son against her, blames her for his excessive drinking, scolds her for mourning the death of her father and refuses to allow her to attend the funeral, brings other drunks into their home who act abhorrently, jokes with his friends that any of them can "have" Helen if they like,[29] gives their young son alcohol, and burns her personal belongings. In sum, Brontë's depiction of this awful marriage through Helen's diary is unflinching despite the scandalous material it contains. The "wholesome truths" Brontë presents are the myriad ways a woman in a bad marriage can experience physical, psychological, and financial harm. In reading Helen's own account of this marriage, we witness those effects firsthand and feel alongside her the crushing weight of Arthur's abuse and dissipation. This makes the documentary form fitting for Brontë's subject matter and challenges the comfortable notion that realist novels best capture the sometimes troubling dynamics of the domestic sphere.

Even in moments when Helen is not the direct victim of Arthur's selfish and manipulative behavior, she observes conduct that reinforces the horrors of male dominance. In one heart-rending scene, when she and Arthur are hosting some of his guests, Ralph Hattersley notices that his wife, Milicent, is crying, and demands to know why. Milicent, clearly too terrified to be honest, refuses to answer him. He grows increasingly agitated, and Milicent warns him, "Do let me alone Ralph! Remember that we are not at home."—A disturbing plea since it suggests that she is accustomed to this treatment, and possibly worse, in the privacy of their home. He replies, "'No matter: you *shall* answer my question!' … and he attempted to extort the confession by shaking her and remorselessly crushing her slight arms in the gripe of his powerful fingers."[30] Ralph's temper continues to escalate, and once his wife finally admits to her reason for crying, he calls her "an impertinent huzzy" and then throws her "with such violence that she [falls] on her side."[31] This scene would be distressing for anyone to witness, but what makes it so awful for Helen is that following Ralph's humiliating and violent treatment of Milicent, Arthur cannot stop laughing. Although Helen has not been the primary target of abuse in this scene, she has witnessed her husband sanction this kind of behavior with his laughter. Arthur's laughter at Milicent's abuse communicates to Helen that he could just as easily laugh at her pain and suffering, and Brontë's writing of this scene, with all of its attending horrors, underscores her desire for readers to recognize the number of ways Helen is demeaned in this marriage—not just by Arthur's actions towards her directly but also by the environment of intimidation and belittling that he fosters in their home. Helen writes in her diary after Arthur comes to bed that night, "sick and stupid" with alcohol, "Such disgraceful scenes (or nearly such) have been repeated more than once."[32] At this point in their marriage Helen's torments are wide-ranging and frequent.

Another troubling scene of male dominance further underscores Brontë's desire to faithfully render the secret "abuses of society" in *The*

Tenant of Wildfell Hall. After Helen has decided to leave her husband and take their son with her, she reveals her intention to Walter Hargrave who then begs her to let him help her. "'Helen! let *me* protect you!'" he cries, adding, "'God has designed me to be your comfort and protector—I feel it—I know it as certainly as if a voice from heaven declared, "Ye twain shall be one flesh.""'[33] Despite Helen's "recoiling" from him and repeated refusals, Hargrave persists. Although he positions himself as if he is asking her permission to act, saying, "'Let me'" and "'give me the power,'" he ultimately demands that she submit to him: "'I lay my powers at your feet—and you must and shall accept them!' he exclaimed impetuously, starting to his feet. 'I *will* be your consoler and defender! and if your conscience upbraid you for it, say I overcame you and you could not choose but yield!'" What Hargrave threatens here is rape, however he might paint himself as someone wanting to help. His threat of sexual violence is clear enough to Helen, who picks up her palette-knife in self-defense. Hargrave, finally yielding to Helen's emphatic verbal and physical refusals, angrily maligns her, saying, "'you are the most cold-hearted, unnatural, ungrateful woman I ever yet beheld.'"[34] Helen's oppression as a miserable wife is such that even an ally threatens her with sexual violence, and Brontë's inclusion of this alarming scene helps make sure that readers understand without a doubt why Helen wants to escape. Men completely dominate the sphere in which she exists, so she must do all she can to leave and take her vulnerable child with her.

Critics have frequently scoffed at the idea that Gilbert reads Helen's diary with all of these troubling scenes and then transcribes it word for word to Halford, but their focus on the novel's logistical authenticity misses the point. Brontë, as her own words attest, wished realistically to depict the ways of "vice and vicious" people, and she uses the epistolary form as a narrative vehicle suited to disclosing individual experiences, promoting private and personal reflection, and embodying social critique.[35] Following his reading of Helen's diary, Gilbert must reflect upon his thoughts and actions with the knowledge of Helen's past experiences. Although he is selfishly disappointed that the diary section Helen has given him ends where it does ("How cruel—just when she was going to mention me!"), he quickly recognizes, "Well, I could readily forgive her prejudice against me, and her hard thoughts of our sex in general, when I saw to what brilliant specimens her experience had been limited."[36] Gilbert, because he has read Helen's diary, must now come to terms with the fact that Helen deeply distrusts men with good reason. On the whole, Gilbert has been self-centered in his pursuit of Helen—a posture effectively embodied in his one-sided, non-dialogic letters and evidenced by his sharing of Helen's private story with a male friend he has disappointed. His swerves of feeling are so distinct and his attachment to Helen so intense that he struggles to see her situation with nuance, but, confronted with the abuse narrated in Helen's diary, Gilbert and we as readers must reevaluate what we thought we knew about the mysterious tenant of Wildfell Hall. The epistolary frame of the novel accentuates Gilbert's transformation upon learning about Helen's past, his remorse at having misjudged her, and his pain at Helen's refusal to continue their relationship while she remains married to Arthur.

Furthermore, the epistolary frame places Helen's private, painful experiences captured in the diary into stark relief against the provincial life and customs of Gilbert's social world. Even though Helen has escaped with her son from her husband, she has not escaped the laws of God and man, nor the judgment of a society that raises girls "to be tenderly and delicately nurtured like a hot-house plant—taught to cling to others for direction and support, and guarded, as much as possible, from the very knowledge of evil," and thus keeps girls "unarmed against her foes."[37] The hybridity of the novel, which some readers have found jarring with its shift in document type, perspective, location, and cast of characters, ultimately helps Brontë emphasize the damage done by English education and marriage customs. The jarring disconnect that readers experience when shifting from Gilbert's retrospective, self-centered narrative to Helen's secret, moving, play-by-play diary does not constitute a fatal structural flaw in Brontë's novel. Rather, as N. M. Jacobs poses, "that displacement is exactly the point of the novel, which subjects its readers to a shouldering-aside of familiar notions and comfortable perceptions of the world."[38] In reading *The Tenant of Wildfell Hall*,

> we approach a horrific private reality only after passing through and then discarding the perceptual structures of a narrator—significantly, a male narrator—who represents the public world that makes possible and tacitly approves the excesses behind the closed doors of these pre-Victorian homes. This structure ...

serves several functions that are strongly gender-related: it exemplifies a process, necessary for both writer and reader, of passing through or going behind the official version of reality in order to approach a truth that the culture prefers to deny; it exemplifies the ways in which domestic reality is obscured by layers of conventional ideology; and it replicates a cultural split between male and female spheres that is shown to be at least one source of the tragedy at the center of the fictional world.[39]

Gilbert's letters, then, help us observe Helen as he did: first as an outsider about whom people gossip, and then as an object of affection whose unwillingness to cave to his advances boggles his mind. The rift between Gilbert and his society's expectations and Helen's experiences and exile emphasizes the burden placed on women in abusive marriages.

While the narrative vehicle of letters is indeed logistically strained (would Gilbert actually write down this much material?), Brontë wants readers to encounter Helen first as a neighborhood oddity whose differences from social norms appropriately appear in documents serving a social function and that in this case work to heal a relationship between men. This structure around Helen's narrative heightens the material nested therein by revealing the dangerous depths to which men may sink when they take full advantage of their superior legal, financial, and social positions in their relationships with women. Furthermore, as many critics have noted, Gilbert's reading, transcribing, and sharing of Helen's diary entries highlights the weight of male authority in this society. Gilbert misunderstands Helen's rejections, and although he is thankfully enlightened by her private diary accounts, he uses her recorded trauma to mend a relationship with a friend. The nested structure of the novel, with its encompassing letter from a man's perspective, underscores Helen's restricted position as a woman, wife, and survivor of domestic violence. While Gilbert is undoubtedly a better husband for Helen than Arthur, this does not mean he exists as a hero outside of his culture, and Brontë's novel persuasively conveys patriarchy's flagrant and pernicious power.[40]

Brontë was aware of the novel's structural discordances, as she reveals in her "Preface," using two metaphors to describe the act of reading her novel:

> But as the priceless treasure too frequently hides at the bottom of a well, it needs some courage to dive for it, especially as he that does so will be likely to incur more scorn and obloquy for the mud and water into which he has ventured to plunge, than thanks for the jewel he procures; as, in like manner, she who undertakes the cleansing of a careless bachelor's apartment will be liable to more abuse for the dust she raises, than commendation for the clearance she effects.[41]

While she does not explicitly reference her letter-framed diary structure here, her descriptions of a diver in the well, making his way through muddy water for hidden treasure, and the housekeeper, making her way through the dirt and grime of "a careless bachelor's apartment," suggest her awareness of the task she has placed on her readers to move from a provincial epistolary novel to a woman's carefully and honestly documented horrors and back again. Brontë also certainly meant to defend herself against critics who found her novel's subject matter objectionable, considering the telling of Helen's story of marital abuse mud and dust, better to remain undisturbed.

Reviewers of *The Tenant of Wildfell Hall* castigated Brontë for her depiction of an abusive relationship, which she saw as an honest depiction of "vice and vicious characters … as they really are."[42] One anonymous reviewer in *Sharpe's London Magazine* wrote

> indeed, so revolting are many of the scenes, so coarse and disgusting the language … that the reviewer to whom we entrusted it returned it to us, saying it was unfit to be noticed in the pages of *Sharpe*; and we are so far of the same opinion, that our object in the present paper is to warn our readers, and more especially our lady-readers, against being induced to peruse it, either by the powerful interest of the story, or the talent with which it is written.[43]

This writer's revulsion at the subject matter weighs so heavily that despite acknowledging that *The Tenant of Wildfell Hall* is both interesting and well-written, the reviewer decides to warn people against picking it up.

The words most often repeated in reviews of Brontë's novel are "coarse" or "coarseness," meaning these readers considered her writing "indecent" and "obscene."[44] Charlotte Brontë seemed to agree, writing to W. S. Williams in 1850 that the novel "hardly appears to me desirable to preserve. The choice of subject in that work is a mistake."[45] As was the case with the publications of all the Brontë sisters, reviewers considered their book's subject matter in relation to the question of their gender, making a judgment about Acton Bell's true identity based on the writer's choice of subject and presentation of it. The same reviewer from *Sharpe's London Magazine*, who considered *The Tenant of Wildfell Hall* unfit for review or readership, develops a rather convoluted theory about Acton Bell's gender identity based on the novel writing,

> At first glance we should say, none but a man could have known so intimately each vile, dark fold of the civilized brute's corrupted nature; none but a man could make so daring an exhibition as this book presents to us. On the other hand, no man, we should imagine, would have written a work in which all the women, even the worst, are so far superior in every quality, moral and intellectual, to all the men; no man would have made his sex appear at once coarse, brutal, and contemptibly weak, at once disgusting and ridiculous. There are, besides, a thousand trifles which indicate a woman's mind, and several more important things which show a woman's peculiar virtues. Still there is a bold coarseness, a reckless freedom of language, and an apparent familiarity with the sayings and doings of the worst style of *fast* men, in their worst moments, which would induce us to believe it impossible that a woman could have written it. A possible solution of the enigma is, that it may be the production of an authoress assisted by her husband, or some other *male* friend: if this be not the case, we would rather decide on the whole, that it is a man's writing.[46]

This roundabout evaluation of the text reveals that this reader has no idea what to make of it, concluding that, ultimately, he would like to believe the book to have been written by a man—an evaluation that seems to be the safest, although still troubling, assessment to the reviewer.

These reviews indicate, in part, the challenges Brontë faced in crafting a novel about such muddy and dusty material as a disastrous marriage. Charles Kingsley wrote in *Fraser's Magazine*, "The author, tempted naturally to indulge her full powers of artistic detail, seems to have forgotten that there are silences more pathetic than all words."[47] But silence is what Brontë was trying to break: her society's silence about what the horrors of male dominance can look like and how the ideal of women as the self-sacrificing moral teachers of men too often place them at the mercy of their husbands. These reviews, although negative, help show why the epistolary mode suited Brontë's controversial subject matter and her desire to be faithful to it, because as Brontë sought to break silence, she did so in fictionalized documents associated with secrecy, private revelations, and intimate social connections. Carol Senf writes that Brontë "adopts a narrative structure that focuses on the way that women's views on such subjects are usually silenced."[48] We only learn about Helen's secret past when she passes a section of her diary to Gilbert in order to prove that he is "mistaken in his conclusions" about her.[49] In doing so, she asks for his loyalty, saying, "don't breathe a word of what it tells you to any living being—I trust to your honour."[50] When Gilbert writes to Halford in an act of atonement, he writes while he is "alone in [his] library," ready to describe for his brother-in-law "a full and faithful account of certain circumstances connected with the most important event of my life."[51] These characters, Helen and Gilbert, share the secrets of their lives in mediums associated with intimacy and privacy. As readers continue to digest *The Tenant of Wildfell Hall* and its coarse subject matter, they should do so with an eye to how Brontë works within the epistolary form to faithfully represent painful truths usually kept secret.

An Englishwoman's Love-Letters

Laurence Housman's epistolary novel *An Englishwoman's Love-Letters* (1900) differs significantly from *The Tenant of Wildfell Hall* and serves as a useful counterpoint to Brontë's novel in a study of documentary fiction that highlights the affordances of this kind of writing. While *The Tenant of Wildfell Hall* has inspired critical debate in Victorian scholarship, *Love-Letters* has enjoyed no such attention. Housman's novel is out of print, and the scholarly record on his work is virtually blank. A thorough examination of this wildly popular turn-of-the-century epistolary novel, however, and consideration of it in comparison to Brontë's text, provides an opportunity to consider the ways different writers approached this form and mined its potentialities in divergent ways.[52] In particular, unlike the letters of *The Tenant of Wildfell Hall*, which are logistically implausible, the letters of Housman's novel closely resemble real correspondence, and his book benefited significantly from the literary climate in which it was published. While Brontë's novel was disparaged widely in the press because of its disturbing subject matter and strained premise, Housman's novel was energetically debated because of the mysteries surrounding its publication and because of recent discussions about the ethics of publishing private materials. *Love-Letters*, although little-known today, deserves attention in this study because it shows the flexibility of the epistolary form and its ability to speak to a particular cultural moment well beyond 1800, the year of its supposed demise.

Love-Letters underscores the possibilities of the epistolary form's artificial premise, as the novel draws attention to itself as a collection of "genuine" letters. Unlike *The Tenant of Wildfell Hall* which uses letters as a framing device, a way into the explosive subject matter, *Love-Letters* uses one woman's correspondence as the narrative vehicle entirely and contains frequent references to the act of letter-writing itself. Whereas Gilbert in *The Tenant of Wildfell Hall* rarely addresses his reader and uses so much dialogue that his writing seems a far cry from actual correspondence, the unnamed Englishwoman of Housman's novel regularly addresses her correspondent and alludes to the logistics of writing and sending letters. She opens and closes each letter (eighty-six in all) with conventional salutations and valedictions, regularly references received correspondence from her "Beloved," describes the time, occasion, or mood of her writing, exhibits an awareness of how her writing may be received and interpreted, describes materials shared between the two writers like books and poems, notes the time gaps between letters, mentions letters that get lost or delayed, and implores her lover to reply in writing and in his visits to her. In short, the reader never thinks that they are reading anything but an Englishwoman's love letters. While Brontë chose to forego any kind of logistical reality in her letters, choosing instead to mine the epistolary form for its impression of emotional and clandestine intimacy, Housman's novel relies heavily on the supposed premise of epistolary fiction: that these are real letters from a real person. The woman's descriptions of her writing consistently remind us of what we hold in our hands. For example, she writes, "So with the sun still a long way out of bed, I have to tuck up these sheets for you" and "Dearest,—Do I not write you long letters?" and "I fear my last letter to you from Lucerne may either have strayed, or not even have begun straying: for in the hurry of coming away I left it, addressed, I *think*, but unstamped."[53] In *The Tenant of Wildfell Hall*, Brontë takes advantage of the letter's *associations* with privacy and intimacy without composing realistic letters; in *Love-Letters*, Housman composes realistic letters and takes advantage of the material qualities of postal communication to make the collection seem genuine. In this respect, we might call it a more traditional epistolary novel than *The Tenant of Wildfell Hall* because of its clear commitment to mimicry of real correspondence. In *The Art of Fiction*, David Lodge describes how this kind of mimicry is unique to epistolary novels:

> Writing, strictly speaking, can only faithfully imitate other writing. Its representation of speech, and still more of non-verbal events, is highly artificial. But a fictional letter is indistinguishable from a real letter. A reference to the circumstances in which a novel is being written, in the text itself, would normally draw attention to the existence of the "real" author behind the text, and thus break the fictional illusion of reality, but in the epistolary novel it contributes to the illusion.[54]

Housman establishes this illusion of reality in a number of ways. First, the novel was published with ornate binding and silk ties suggesting that the book's contents derived from a young woman's private materials, and the volume did not include Housman's name anywhere. In his autobiography, *The Unexpected Years* (1937), Housman writes that the decision to leave his name off the book was a necessity "since a woman's love-letters followed by a man's name on the title-page would have looked absurd."[55] Second, he opens the novel with an "Explanation" in which an unidentified editor describes the circumstances of the publication and highlights the ways these letters fulfill Cooke's promise of letter-writing's value in terms of their secrecy and faithfulness. He writes,

> It need hardly be said that the woman by whom these letters were written had no thought that they would be read by any one but the person to whom they were addressed. But a request, conveyed under circumstances which the writer herself would have regarded as all-commanding, urges that they should now be given to the world: and, so far as is possible with a due regard to the claims of privacy, what is here printed presents the letters as they were first written in their complete form and sequence.[56]

Like Samuel Richardson in his preface to *Clarissa*, the fictional editor describes and defends editorial decisions, including changing "A few names of persons and localities ... and several short notes (not above twenty in all), together with some passages bearing too intimately upon events which might be recognised, have been left out without indication of their omission."[57] The letters, therefore, seem legitimate not only because of their likeness to actual love letters but also because they have supposedly been edited with care by an unknown but respectful and respectable hand. The editor poses as a conscientious handler of the book's delicate and private contents, writing, "The story which darkens these pages cannot be more fully indicated while the feelings of some who are still living have to be consulted."[58] This editorial posturing conveys a sense of faithfulness and respect toward the material. In addition to the editorial note that attempts to legitimate the letters, Housman believed at the time that his publisher's solid reputation would also "guarantee authenticity" of the book.[59] In other words, not only did the book's contents and appearance suggest legitimacy, but the name of John Murray on the title page, the publishing house of such luminaries as Walter Scott, Lord Byron, Jane Austen, and Charles Darwin, also bestowed a level of prestige that conveyed credibility.[60]

Housman knew that establishing credibility was crucial to his book having any resonance with readers. Unlike *The Tenant of Wildfell Hall*, in which Brontë might retain reader interest by building suspense around the mysterious past of Helen and through the unfolding love story of she and Gilbert, *Love-Letters* depends substantially on readers believing the collection to be genuine. According to Housman, "had my authorship been discovered, [the book's] main interest would have gone."[61] Housman does not claim his novel has other qualities that deserve reader attention or critical interest. In contrast to Brontë, he does not claim to be presenting the truth about vile people or addressing an abuse of society. Rather, Housman states that he created something whose primary feature was its premise, its forgery.

The illusion worked. Many readers and reviewers thought the correspondence genuine, in contrast to reviewers of *The Tenant of Wildfell Hall* who found the epistolary frame entirely implausible and questionable even as a narrative technique. Despite the "Explanation" that opens the book, unexplained details regarding the public release of the letters and the mysterious cause of the couple's separation engendered debate among readers and heightened interest in the text. The plot of *Love-Letters* is fairly simple. A young woman regularly writes to her beloved suitor about her love for him, their engagement, her travels, and her hopes for their future. Looming over these sentimental messages, however, is the man's mother who has expressed, so we are told, criticism of the match. Ultimately, the woman's beloved breaks off the relationship in a short letter to her, without explanation for his action except that she is not at "fault."[62] Miserable and ill, she continues to write letters to him that she does not post until she dies at the young age of twenty-two, unvisited and hardly acknowledged by her former lover. Because of the man's unsatisfying reasons for breaking off the relationship, the mysterious motives for publishing the letters, and the woman's tragic death, readers debated numerous aspects of the collection, including what could have been the unspoken prohibition that separated the lovers and the ethics of sharing such personal materials with the public.

Reviews and letters to editors following the book's publication capture these debates and reveal how Housman creatively took advantage of public interest in private romantic correspondence. The initial review published in *The Academy: A Weekly Review of Literature and Life* on December 1 does not question the authenticity of the collection (Housman had faked it well) but compliments the woman's writing style and ability to disclose "her innermost feelings in a way that makes even a reviewer blush to think that he has been peeping and prying into intimate confessions."[63] The reviewer concludes that the cause of the couple's split was "that this gentleman was not able to live up to the passion of his correspondent" and that the Englishwoman "loved too well, too unwisely well, and she paid for her excess" in her pathetic death.[64] Certainly, Housman's decision to construct the book from *a woman's letters rather than a couple's letters* contribute to this sense that the relationship was fatally one-sided. The woman's declarations of love are frequently hyperbolic, and the monologic nature of the book accentuates this as we do not read similar professions of love from the man. We get exclamations from her like, "I am yours so utterly," and "[I] am merely a very helpless loving nonentity which merges itself most happily in you," and "you are my share of the world, also my share of Heaven,"[65] but, not being given direct access to any of his replies, readers do not know if he shares this kind of exuberance in his love for her.

The *Academy* reviewer sees the one-sided nature of this attachment as not only a personal weakness of the woman, whose love is excessive, but also a weakness of the publication, which lacks a balanced perspective. To carry the point, the reviewer compares the collection to the recently published love letters of the Brownings: "We miss the larger utterance, the interest in life itself, in life's crowded interests of which love, if the best and the most helpful, is but one. We miss the fine understanding of the proportions of things which distinguished the Browning love-letters."[66] This reference to the Brownings' correspondence is intriguing for a couple of reasons. First, it underscores Housman's success in passing off "that surreptitious fake, the *Love-letters*" as genuine correspondence,[67] and second, it positions Housman's book as a competitor to *The Letters of Robert Browning and Elizabeth Barrett Barrett, 1845–1846*, which were published in two volumes the previous year. Reviews of the Browning collection upon its publication express deep admiration for the poets, their intelligent discussions of literature and philosophy, and their modest yet ardent love for each other. The *Saturday Review* claims,

> We have read [the letters] with great care, with growing aston-
> ishment, with immense respect; and the final result produced on
> our minds, by what has been really rather a heavy piece of mental

work, is that these volumes contain one of the most precious contributions to literary history which our time has seen. They are not "amusing," there is little progress of plot, they make a poor novel in correspondence … But for solid value as a contribution to psychology, as a revelation of the inmost thoughts and impulses of two noble natures, for the wholesomeness of their display of simplicity, unselfishness, and goodness of heart, interpreted in the finest literary medium, we do not, for the moment, recollect anything to parallel these letters of R.B. and E.B.B.[68]

Although the *Academy* reviewer does not believe *An Englishwoman's Love-Letters* lives up to the Browning collection in terms of its value, both reviews praise the collections for some of the same qualities, including their ability to convey "inmost thoughts." Like the reviewer of *Love-Letters* in *The Academy*, the critic of the Browning's letters in *The Athenæum* describes the exhilarating yet deviant sense one gets engaging the material: "in reading them one feels almost a sense of shame, as if one were prying on a mystery which can only be fully intelligible to those actually taking part in it at the moment."[69] Housman's great success in his novel is achieving this same sense of keyhole access. His readers, like those of the Browning letters, are titillated by the idea that they have gained admission to such private thoughts and pledges of affection.

In addition to noting the voyeuristic element of reading another person's love letters, the reviews of the Browning's real collection and Housman's artificial one debate the ethics of publishing private materials. The publication of Housman's novel on the heels of the success of the Browning's legitimate, although controversial, collection suggests that his book was able to take advantage of this cultural moment in which the literary world was enthralled and divided by the publication of such letters. Despite nearly universal agreement that the Browning letters are wonderful to read and fascinating to behold, many reviewers questioned the couple's son for deciding to publish the correspondence. The *Athenæum* reviewer writes,

Mr. Browning says that his father left these letters to him with the injunction to do with them as he pleased when the writer was dead and gone. We should like to think that Browning never conceived the possibility of his son's publishing them; but, even if he had such an unexpressed idea, more honour would have been done to a great poet's memory by destroying them than by allowing it for a moment to be thought that he sanctioned their publication.[70]

The *Saturday Review* took the counter position, siding strongly with the decision of the son to publish, believing that his father would have destroyed the letters himself if he truly did not want any other eyes to see them, and citing the letters' unique literary qualities and the way they exonerate the couple's decision to marry secretly and flee to Italy.[71] A lengthy article in the *Edinburgh Review* takes this debate over publication as its primary subject. The article, titled "Discretion and Publicity," begins, "What should be put into print? What withheld?" and then continues for six pages explaining why this kind of correspondence should not be published, claiming that "love letters, as a general rule, have no business with print."[72] Six pages into this argument, however, the writer declares that the Brownings are the one exception to this rule because their love story is "the most wonderful ... that the world knows of" and is so central to their poetic work.[73] Despite the "besetting sense of eavesdropping" and "a really regrettable precedent" the Browning letters might establish, the writer concludes: "[I]t is all but imperative for the credit of humanity that this story should be told"—perhaps with a bit more editing to preserve some privacy—but, ultimately, "[W]e cannot wish this record of their love inaccessible."[74]

These reviews and their different positions on the ethics of publishing private correspondence indicate both public interest and concern over these kinds of publications, and this was the context into which Housman inserted his epistolary novel, his fake collection of love letters. It suggests that he not only worked to take advantage of the conventions of letter writing in his novel, giving readers supposedly faithful, secret, and social correspondence, but that he also took advantage of a literary climate that was both fascinated and troubled by these kinds of books.[75] A letter written to *The Academy* by a reader of Housman's *Love-Letters*, and published in its December 15 issue, documents this climate, saying that the book is a very skilful appeal to the present appetite for "interiors," which the publication of Mrs. Browning's letters seems to have whetted amazingly. The heroine is dragged into view, stripped bare for inspection, and then (lest we should doubt her flesh and blood) flayed alive before our eyes; we touch at once the zenith of sensationalism and the nadir of decency; and the pity of it is that "even the very elect are deceived" into approval.[76]

This "present appetite for 'interiors'" gave Housman a primed audience, interested (even when upset by its sensationalism and indecency) in private, romantic correspondence. Readers wanted, sometimes in spite of themselves, access to *the real*, and Housman's book provided it to them through these fake letters. The novelist believed *Love-Letters* to be "the worst book [he] ever wrote," but his decision to create a collection that could pass as real, titillated readers with access to privileged information, and raised questions about its origin earned him more money than anything else he had written.[77] And he was right that the "main interest" of his book was its anonymity. The mystery surrounding the letters' authenticity and authorship inspired debate, and copycats and spinoffs were able to cash in on the lack of author attribution.[78] Once the news broke that Housman had written *Love-Letters*, the book's status waned, Housman moved on with his career, and the canon mostly forgot the volume with its pretty green silk ties.

Despite the novel's passage into historical and literary obscurity, the popularity of Housman's novel when it was published and the debates it spurred illustrate that readers still found the epistolary novel an engaging medium even at the *fin de siècle*, one hundred years after the epistolary novel was declared dead. Housman's cleverness lies not only in his presentation of this woman's heartbreak through realistic letters but also in the way he seems to have taken advantage of a cultural moment in which people questioned the line between public and private and were attracted to texts that toyed with that boundary line.

In fact, we see in both novels a meaningful desire to play with or, at least, explore the appropriate boundary between public and private. Housman's novel clearly exploits turn-of-the-century readers' enthusiasm for seemingly authentic, exclusive, and engrossing private, romantic correspondence. The confusion and debate over the source of the letters, their authenticity, and the ethics of publishing love letters undoubtedly contributed to the book's popularity. In a similar vein, Brontë scholars continue to wrestle with Gilbert's transcription of Helen's diary into correspondence with his friend, making her private accounts of abuse public. This shared dynamic between *The Tenant of Wildfell Hall* and *An Englishwoman's Love-Letters* is significant because, as already noted, the epistolary novel has been repeatedly termed a dead mode of writing. The letter's capacity, however, to serve as a literary vehicle for inquiries into issues of privacy, access, and authenticity, as I hope I have shown, make it especially *modern* rather than archaic. After all, ours is an era when social media feeds present images, videos, and text that purportedly provide unadulterated access to our friends', colleagues', and public figures' private lives. How much of that is real? How much is edited for public consumption? How much is created purely to entice followers addicted to a sense of access? How much is appropriate to reveal? And is it okay to watch and share? Accordingly, Brontë's and Housman's novels, as different as they are, show us the underrecognized capacities of the epistolary novel and its contemporary purchase in a globalized twenty-first century addicted to technology that consistently provides access to and correspondence with the private sphere.

CHAPTER TWO

Life-Writing Novels

Defining Life-Writing Documentary Novels

Here we encounter a heavily populated branch on the family tree of Victorian documentary novels. In this chapter, I describe the family traits and key affordances of life-writing documentary novels, how they are distinguishable from first-person novels, and place this book in conversation with recent scholarship on life writing—particularly Heidi L. Pennington's *Creating Identity in the Victorian Fictional Autobiography* (2018) and Desirée Henderson's *How to Read a Diary: Critical Contexts and Interpretive Strategies for 21st-Century Readers* (2019). In covering this ground, I highlight the formal qualities of several Victorian life-writing documentary novels, including Thomas Carlyle's *Sartor Resartus* (1834), William Makepeace Thackeray's *The Memoirs of Barry Lyndon, Esq.* (1844), Anne Brontë's *Agnes Grey* (1847), Charlotte Brontë's *Jane Eyre* (1847), and Charles Dickens's *David Copperfield* (1850). I situate these five novels on a spectrum, according to the ways they utilize the affordances of this constraining documentary form. Although they all fit under the subgenre of life-writing documentary novels, the texts differ substantially in their messages about society, identity, and the ability of a narrative to encapsulate a person's experiences and sense of self. Accordingly, I show how the constraining premise of authentic personal documents allows novelists more creative latitude than we might expect.

Before describing why these novels land on the spectrum where they do, it is important to define some terms and categories because life-writing documentary novels consist of several related forms that are nonetheless distinct from one another. These may be novels written and labeled as supposedly authentic autobiographies, biographies, memoirs, personal papers, diaries, or journals. Except for biography novels, which are fairly rare, these novels are written in the first person and feature a writer–protagonist. On the one hand, most of the novels I discuss in this book could be termed life writing because they feature central characters writing about their lives. The travel and adventure novels covered in the next chapter, for instance, feature writer–protagonists who narrate their own lived experiences, but the scope of these novels is limited to the events of a single journey and a short period in the life of the individual.[1] Similarly, in the casebook novels discussed in Chapter 4, while the narrators describe events from their lives, their contributions pertain to a particular event or related series of events, and they play a specified role in building or preserving a case. In other words, the subject matter is not one person's life broadly understood. Rather, the subject is the mystery, crime, or villain, and these pieces of life writing are collected to address those circumstances. In *Dracula* (1897), for example, personal papers like journal entries are included, but the subject of the novel is the collective effort to defeat an invading monster. Mina, Jonathan, and friends write about themselves and their experiences, but the "mass of typewriting" collected by Mina documents the group's struggle to understand and then defeat their enemy.[2] The documents are not about who they are or who they become as people. Once the enemy is defeated, the novel ends.

By contrast, life-writing novels as I define them are not limited to the period of a particular adventure or terrifying trial; they may cover more everyday domestic life, and they may cover a large span of years. I use the terms autobiography, biography, memoir, personal papers, diaries, and journals in the same way they are used to label works of non-fiction, and I use them because these novelists label their books as such. However, because some of these terms get used interchangeably in both popular and academic discourse, I will offer some definitions here, building on the work of scholars in the field of life writing.

While "*autobiography*" and "*memoir*" are often used interchangeably, scholars and writers do differentiate between them. Both consist of reflective writing about one's life, although an autobiography typically covers "an extended period of some person's life, written by, or presented as having been written by, that person."[3] This contrasts with a memoir that may cover only certain years or a particular event in a person's life. A memoir may focus more on other people, and it may be more episodic and less "tied to the personal development of the narrator."[4] In *Creating Identity in the Victorian Fictional Autobiography*, Pennington identifies "three thematic focuses" of autobiographies that further illuminate the distinctions between autobiography, memoir, and first-person novels more generally. She writes:

> Autobiographies of the nineteenth century demonstrate (1) an investment in the narrator's origins and development, particularly in his childhood and education; (2) a desire to represent an individual self, with the attendant if often implied stipulation that it be an expression of an essential self; and (3) a desire for—sometimes becoming a rhetorical insistence upon—social recognition of that self's worth and authenticity. I refer to these three thematic focuses as origins, self-representation, and social recognition of the self.[5]

As Pennington makes clear, Victorian autobiographies do not merely share characteristics in terms of point of view and form, they also share characteristics in terms of content. These books, and their fictional "literary siblings,"[6] as she calls them, dwell on these "three main content concerns."[7] These characteristics, among other things, distinguish fictional autobiographies from other first-person novels that do not share this preoccupation with the writer–protagonist's origins, development, individuality, and social achievement or recognition.[8] Using this metric, Pennington claims Charlotte Brontë's *Jane Eyre* and Charles Dickens's *David Copperfield* are prime examples of fictional autobiography.[9] Both novels present "a first-person, retrospective account of the imaginary narrating protagonist's life story; this life story is self-consciously told" and "[t]he interest of their tales lies in the elaboration and validation of the identity of the character-narrator."[10] By highlighting the fact that not all first-person novels share these concerns about development and identity, Pennington demonstrates that while *autobiographical writing* is often used as a broad, umbrella term, *life writing* more accurately defines a range of related subgenres, of which autobiographies are one.

Pennington's emphasis on the distinct content of autobiographies, fictional and non-fictional, also helpfully demarcates them from documentary novels written as personal papers, diaries, and journals. Although novelists have used these terms to label their works of fiction, like Dickens's *The Posthumous Papers of the Pickwick Club Containing a Faithful Record of the Perambulations, Perils, Travels, Adventures and Sporting Transactions of the Corresponding Members* (1837), George and Weedon Grossmith's *The Diary of a Nobody* (1892), and Emma Marshall's *Mrs. Mainwaring's Journal* (1874), generally speaking, novelists' applications of these terms are inconsistent and sometimes at odds with how readers or critics might define them.[11] Furthermore, many novels lack this kind of labeling in their title but nonetheless fit these descriptions in terms of form. Recognizing this instability of terms, I follow Desirée Henderson in using *"diary"* as a broad term that includes "a wide range of writing styles, authorial personas, and individual, social and political goals."[12] Although I previously listed personal papers, diaries, and journals separately, Henderson advocates for all of these novels to be termed *"diary fiction."* She prefers the term *"diary"* to *"journal"* because the latter "has so many different meanings (referring to periodicals and newspapers, for instance) that it is not particularly useful as a search term" and because she wants to "[recover] the word [diary] and the genre it describes from its status as a feminized, minimized, and even shameful form of writing."[13] Diary fiction, then, includes novels taking the form of regular or semi-regular entries of retrospective yet often in-the-moment writing or in-the-immediate-aftermath writing. This helps distinguish them from fictional autobiographies, which, although also retrospective, typically have a broader view or stance. As Catherine Delafield writes in *Women's Diaries as Narrative in the Nineteenth-Century Novel*, "The diary presents the unmediated reflection of a life without interpretation whilst autobiography overwrites a life already lived with knowledge of narrative closure."[14] Diary novels may contain significant formal constraints if the novelist chooses to retain conventional features of non-fiction diary writing like dating or time stamping, additional space between entries, writing errors and corrections, a chronological structure, and an attentiveness to "the present moment."[15] Or, as Trevor Field describes them in *Form and Function in the Diary Novel*, these books "[draw] attention to an on-going present where different days are observable or implied."[16] But novelists may also choose to use the diary premise only as a launching-off point or as a simple claim to authenticity—at which point, as Henderson writes, they "give up the pretense that they are diaries in order to take advantage of more conventional and flexible storytelling modes."[17]

In sum, I use *"life-writing documentary novels"* to refer to a number of forms that are narrated entirely by means of a supposed autobiography, memoir, diary, or biography. Following Henderson, I use the term *"diary"* to include narratives labeled as personal papers and journals. What this mixture of terms should suggest is this branch of the family tree is rather crowded and tangled. Life-writing novels include a fascinating variety of texts and levels of engagement with the form. For this reason, I propose placing them on a spectrum that underscores their broad range of affordances. Doing so will not only disentangle some of these novels' differences in terms of stance, form, and audience engagement, but also will clearly illustrate the diversity of this kind of writing in the nineteenth century.

While each type of life-writing novel (fictional autobiographies, memoirs, diaries, and biographies) has affordances unique to its form (see Figure 2.1), they operate these potentialities in varying degrees. On a spectrum of life-writing documentary novels, at one end sit novels that use the form merely as a premise but then largely abandon references to the form in the narrative (Figure 2.2). These novels may, as Henderson claims, read more like conventional first-person novels that do not claim to be authentic documents. At the other end of the spectrum sit novels that are highly self-conscious of their form and may go so far as to manipulate conventional expectations to comment on life writing more broadly. Two Victorian novels will suitably illustrate these extreme ends—Anne Brontë's *Agnes Grey* and Thomas Carlyle's *Sartor Resartus*—and will illuminate the range of affordances of nineteenth-century documentary life writing.

LIFE WRITING DOCUMENTARY NOVELS

fictional autobiographies	cover the writer-protagonist's development over many years
	are retrospective yet convey an awareness of closure
	tend to emphasize individuality and the notion of "an essential self"
	work toward social achievement or recognition
fictional memoirs	tend to be more narrow in scope and subject matter than fictional autobiographies
	may focus more on other people than the supposed writer
	can be episodic and less concerned with the writer's development
fictional diaries	contain regular or semi-regular entries of retrospective writing that can feel "in the moment" or close to it
	may include conventions like dating, time gaps between entries, and writing errors that emphasize authenticity and/or immediacy
	convey intimacy through the reader's seemingly privileged access to the private materials
	may feel more short-sighted than autobiographies and memoirs as the writer-protagonist does not know what will come next
fictional biographies	are less common than other forms of life writing novels
	may contain some of the same thematic concerns that fictional autobiographies do but typically does not feature a first-person narrator

Figure 2.1: Life-writing documentary novels: fictional autobiographies,
fictional memoirs, fictional diaries, and fictional biographies

**SPECTRUM OF LIFE WRITING
DOCUMENTARY NOVELS**

Figure 2.2: Spectrum of life-writing documentary novels:
Agnes Grey, Sartor Resartus

The Ends of the Spectrum: *Agnes Grey* and *Sartor Resartus*

Agnes Grey, published a year before *The Tenant of Wildfell Hall*, opens with a paragraph common to many Victorian documentary novels in which the writer–protagonist makes a claim of authenticity, veracity, and humility.[18] She begins,

> All true histories contain instruction; though, in some, the treasure may be hard to find, and when found, so trivial in quantity that the dry, shriveled kernel scarcely compensates for the trouble of cracking the nut. Whether this be the case with my history or not, I am hardly competent to judge; I sometimes think it might prove useful to some, and entertaining to others, but the world may judge for itself: shielded by my own obscurity, and by the lapse of years, and a few fictitious names, I do not fear to venture, and will candidly lay before the public what I would not disclose to the most intimate friend.[19]

Agnes, the writer–protagonist, claims to present a "true history" that she is not competent enough to judge. She relies, so she says, on the reader to judge for herself whether the book has merits beyond mere triviality. Even more profoundly, she claims that her true history contains material she would not share with even her "most intimate friend." Providing unknown readers a sense of privileged access emphasizes the narrative's value and crafts an illusion of the reader trespassing into highly sensitive territory. In these opening sentences, Brontë imbues her book with a sense of intimacy and authenticity. The protagonist writes from her own lived experiences, tender and salacious enough to warrant name changes and to benefit from the cover of her "obscurity," and this premise and promise of an authentic and credible narrative helps lure readers to build a connection with the novel's narrator from the book's first paragraph.

A premise and promise is largely all it is, though. She does not emphasize the form of the book nor does she make use of conventions that would visually cue readers that they are reading authentic documents of any kind. While Agnes occasionally makes direct addresses to her readers, they typically take an apologetic tone regarding the book's contents rather than offer commentary on the book's form. Her addresses to the reader defend her choices to gloss over or skip certain material. "I spare my readers the account of my delight on coming home," she says in chapter 4.[20] "As I cannot," she confesses in chapter 7, "find it in my heart to bestow *all* my tediousness upon the reader, I will not go on to bore him with a minute detail of all the discoveries and proceedings of this and the following day."[21] At one point she returns to the subject matter of the novel's first paragraph—the issue of content too private for "the most intimate friend"—and acknowledges, "I began this book with the intention of concealing nothing, that those who liked might have the benefit of perusing a fellow creature's heart: but we have *some* thoughts that all the angels in heaven are welcome to behold—but not our brother-men—not even the best and kindest amongst them."[22] We discover the limits, then, of the writer–protagonist's willingness to share her most private thoughts.

These kinds of remarks to the reader are not unusual in life-writing novels, and, in fact, Pennington claims they are crucially important in fictional autobiographies. She writes that "fictional autobiographies fulfill the audience's desire for intimacy with and knowledge of the narrator-protagonists through reader-inclusion strategies that require the audience to take part in the creation of the identities with whom they seek communion."[23] In the case of Agnes Grey, who seeks desperately to be understood and valued by those around her, her apologies and explanations to the reader enhance her honest character as a daughter, governess, and future wife and mother. She invites readers to see her as very few characters in the novel do: a trustworthy, perceptive individual with greater capability than many around her believe. These moments when she addresses the reader, although they draw attention to the constructed nature of the narrative, further solidify her identity and its value—a key goal of a fictional autobiography.

Because of this, it makes more sense to refer to *Agnes Grey* as a fictional autobiography, as Pennington defines it, than as a diary novel, which Agnes herself references. A few paragraphs from the end of the novel, after she and Mr. Weston have professed their love for one another, she writes, "Here I pause. My diary, from which I compiled these pages, goes but little farther. I could go on for years."[24] This revelation concerning the novel's construction is a bit surprising as no reference to a diary has been made before this moment. Garrett Stewart reflects, "25 chapters of harrowing servitude and mistreatment and final conjugal reward later, we hear only at the very close about the means by which this text has in fact been 'laid before the public.'"[25] Although Agnes's description that her text has been "compiled" from the diary is somewhat vague, we are left to presume this means she used it as a reference when drafting her autobiography since the narrative itself does not consist of dated entries and retains a omniscient stance from beginning to end.

Accordingly, I place Brontë's novel on the far-left side of my proposed spectrum of Victorian life-writing documentary novels. I do not mean that she does not take advantage of the affordances of the form, but rather that she does so in a very restricted way. As I already discussed, Brontë develops and coheres her writer–protagonist's identity in *Agnes Grey* by situating her as an honest, inexperienced conveyer of her own experiences, an endeavor in which she recruits readers to participate by explaining her writing choices to them at various points throughout the novel. Her premise that this is a self-written text and promise that it is crafted honestly, with corresponding comments to that effect throughout, usefully enhance what is already the focus of the novel: Agnes as an under-appreciated young woman striving for recognition, stability, and respect. In other words, Brontë makes minimal reference to the documentary form of this novel because that is all she needs to do in order to achieve her desired atmosphere of authenticity, intimacy, and identity formation.

The book on the other side of the spectrum will illuminate Brontë's modest deployment of the affordances of this subgenre of documentary novels. Thomas Carlyle's *Sartor Resartus* is a layered, hybrid work of fiction that has been described as "a work of the foremost literary historical importance,"[26] but also "unclassifiable"[27] and "one of the noisiest books among the classics of English literature."[28] Unlike *Agnes Grey*, which uses the posture of an authentic book of life writing to enhance its subject matter but comments little on its form, Carlyle's book constantly draws attention to its construction and the variety of documents it engages to deliver its "Philosophy of Clothes."[29] *Sartor Resartus* begins straightforwardly enough as an anonymously written review essay fitting for a periodical like *Fraser's Magazine*, but it soon morphs into part book review, part biography, part translation, and part memoir of the supposed Editor's difficulties in working with the German philosopher's materials.[30] Because it is such a hybrid text, one might, like Vanessa L. Ryan, term it "unclassifiable," but it best fits under this category of life-writing fiction because of the way Carlyle uses the book to bring attention to and comment on the project of life writing. In this way he engages the latent potentialities of life-writing documentary fiction quite differently than Brontë, creating a highly self-conscious work of fiction that displays the form's inherent qualities (and, we might say, oddities). In placing *Sartor Resartus* on the other end of the spectrum from *Agnes Grey*, and in emphasizing the ways Carlyle exaggeratingly exploits the affordances of life writing, we will be able to see more clearly the range of ways novelists employ this documentary form.

Like many documentary novels, *Sartor Resartus* has a premise communicated to the reader at the beginning of the text. Here an unnamed Editor reveals his task of bringing the "life and opinions" of a German philosopher named Diogenes Teufelsdröckh before the British public. Teufelsdröckh's book, *Die Kleider ihr Werden und Wirken* ("Clothes, their Origin and Influence"), being "an 'extensive Volume,' of boundless, almost formless contents, a very Sea of Thought; neither calm nor clear," proves difficult for the Editor to translate, understand, or summarize for his British readers.[31] Thus, as Ryan writes, the book becomes "an attempt to translate a system of philosophy by constructing a biography."[32] The Editor hopes that in learning more about Teufelsdröckh's life he will better understand the man's philosophy and thus be able to deliver it "to the business and bosoms of our own English nation."[33] Rather than having this editorial premise recede into the background (to operate as a frame narrative, as happens in many works of documentary fiction), the created Editor of *Sartor Resartus* frequently draws attention to his presence and the difficulty of his job working with Teufelsdröckh's ideas and materials. This foregrounding is made most clear by a chapter wholly devoted to "Editorial Difficulties" near the beginning of the book but is also communicated clearly throughout the entire novel as the Editor regularly interrupts his translations of the philosopher's writing to express frustration and confusion.

A promise of greater understanding arrives early in *Sartor Resartus* when the Editor is contacted by Teufelsdröckh's "chief friend and associate," who informs him "that should the present Editor feel disposed to undertake a Biography of Teufelsdröckh, he, Hofrath Heuschrecke, had it in his power to furnish the requisite Documents."[34] At first this seems to be the moment for which the Editor and his reader have been waiting: the documents! Surely they will reveal the man and his ideas. The Editor describes the promise of these primary materials as "a cheerful daystar of hope" that has bolstered his work so far.[35] Even better, when the documents arrive, the Editor discovers them to be "not a Biography only, but an Autobiography: at least the materials for such."[36] Here Carlyle plays upon our expectations of what life-writing and particularly primary materials can offer. We presume they provide access to the truth and the real person. As Henderson writes about diaries, we expect that as "original manuscripts" they will be privately produced and protected "truthful records."[37]

These primary sources, though, prove tremendously disappointing. They are not a selection of organized files, a collection of journals neatly kept, or an illuminating logbook of activities, readings, and thoughts. Rather, they are six poorly labeled paper bags filled with a jumble of materials. Because Carlyle has so built up the anticipation for what Heuschrecke's delivery will bestow, it is worth quoting at length the Editor's reaction to receiving these materials.

> And now let the sympathizing reader judge of our feeling when, in place of this same Autobiography with "fullest insight," we find—Six considerable PAPER-BAGS, carefully sealed, and marked successively, in gilt China-ink, with the symbols of the Six southern Zodiacal Signs, beginning at Libra; in the inside of which sealed Bags lie miscellaneous masses of Sheets, and oftener Shreds and Snips, written in Professor Teufelsdröckh's scarce-legible *cursiv-schrift*; and treating of all imaginable things under the Zodiac and above it, but of his own personal history only at rare intervals, and then in the most enigmatic manner.[38]

The layers of confusion Carlyle humorously embeds into these bags is considerable. Although the bags are labeled, it is not clear why they are marked with astrological signs or why the labeling begins with Libra, the seventh sign in the zodiac. While the bags do contain manuscript material, they are disorganized, partial, or damaged, and feature illegible handwriting. Not only that, the materials hardly reveal any of the philosopher's "personal history," despite the promise that these documents would provide all that would be needed to write a biography of Teufelsdröckh. Continuing to describe the contents, the Editor writes:

> Whole fascicles there are, wherein the Professor, or, as he here, speaking in the third person, calls himself, "the Wanderer", is not once named. Then again, amidst what seems to be a Metaphysico-theological Disquisition, "Detached Thoughts on the Steam-engine", or, "The continued Possibility of Prophecy", we shall meet with some quite private, not unimportant Biographical fact. On certain sheets stand Dreams, authentic or not, while the circumjacent waking Actions are omitted. Anecdotes, oftenest without date of place or time, fly loosely on separate slips, like Sibylline leaves. Interspersed also are long purely Autobiographical delineations; yet without connexion, without recognizable coherence; so unimportant, so superfluously minute, they almost remind us of "P. P. Clerk of this Parish". Thus does famine of intelligence alternate with waste.[39]

Inside the paper bags are documents in which Teufelsdröckh is referenced by another name in the third person. The titles of the philosophical works included—"Detached Thoughts on the Steam-engine" and "The continued Possibility of Prophecy"—are similarly vague and incomplete, with names suggesting that they should be connected with something else that is not included in the bag. If there is a "continued Possibility of Prophecy," for example, one would expect there to be an originating possibility of it. To add to the confusion, his pieces of autobiographical writing lack any clarity and undated "slips" of paper "fly loosely" about so that the most the Editor can say of the collection is, "Thus does famine of intelligence alternate with waste."

In emphasizing the failure of authentic documents to reveal clear truths or even verifiable patterns of behavior or thinking, Carlyle pushes us to question whether access to the real individual is even possible. As the Editor writes in the "Romance" chapter, "How from such inorganic masses, henceforth madder than ever, as lie in these Bags, can even fragments of a living delineation be organized? Besides, of what profit were it?"[40] While Brontë crafts a writer–protagonist who pledges honesty at the opening of her autobiography, Carlyle creates an Editor who expresses a desire or at least a willingness to faithfully report on "the Life and Opinions of Herr Teufelsdröckh" but who continually faces barriers to his own understanding of this man and his ideas and to his ability to construct a coherent narrative of this person's life and accomplishments. The Editor's exasperations at the German thinker in *Sartor Resartus* are numerous, but a small sampling of his comments illustrates how often Carlyle draws our attention to the tenuously constructed nature of this text. In writing of "the bag *Sagittarius*," the Editor vents, "Few things, in the way of confusion and capricious indistinctness, can now surprise our readers; not even the total want of dates, almost without parallel in a Biographical work." The bag contains "fragments of all sorts; scraps of regular Memoir, College-Exercises, Programs, Professional Testimoniums, Milkscores, torn Billets, sometimes to appearance of an amatory cast; all blown together as if by merest chance, henceforth bewilder the sane Historian."[41] The Editor is perhaps most bewildered a chapter later when he proclaims, "Foolish were it in us to attempt following him, even from afar, in this extraordinary world-pilgrimage of his; the simplest record of which, were clear record possible, would fill volumes. Hopeless is the obscurity, unspeakable the confusion."[42] Brontë's trustworthy writer–protagonist confidently leads us through her experiences, directly addressing readers when she finds it needful to explain content she has excluded from her life's record. In doing so, she underscores her independence, intelligence, and coherent identity—a crucial affordance of life-writing documentary novels. Carlyle's Editor, on the other hand, is made speechless with confusion and almost entirely lacks confidence in the man and the materials with which he works. He even goes so far as to wonder whether this is all a hoax:

> Here, indeed, at length, must the Editor give utterance to a painful suspicion, which, through late Chapters, has begun to haunt him; paralysing any little enthusiasm that might still have rendered his thorny Biographical task a labour of love. It is a suspicion grounded perhaps on trifles, yet confirmed almost into certainty by the more and more discernible humoristico-satirical tendency

of Teufelsdröckh, in whom underground humours, and intricate sardonic rogueries, wheel within wheel, defy all reckoning: a suspicion, in one word, that these Autobiographical Documents are partly a Mystification![43]

Rather than an editor who is confident in the materials he presents to readers, as is the case with many documentary novels, the Editor of Carlyle's novel is dismayed to the point of questioning not only the philosophy of Teufelsdröckh but the very evidence of his life. He asks, "What if many a so-called Fact were little better than a Fiction," and he has been "made a fool"? Crucially, we must observe that Carlyle crafts a book in which the Editor (who is also translator and memoir and biography writer) ironically interrogates the very possibility of writing about a person's life. Furthermore, even when the Editor praises Teufelsdröckh, the Editor conditions his compliments with criticism, as at the end of the book when he writes, "Of Professor Teufelsdröckh it seems impossible to take leave without a mingled feeling of astonishment, gratitude and disapproval."[44]

In these ways, the Editor regularly draws our attention to how the philosopher's documents *should work*, but *never quite do*. What this should show us is that the documentary form of *Sartor Resartus* is as important as its content—indeed *is* its content. Ryan describes this aspect of the book in the following way:

Just as the "unreliable narrator" in late nineteenth-century fiction shifts attention from the story narrated to the mode of narration, the "unreliable editor" of *Sartor Resartus* gives dramatic form to questions of authenticity, veracity, and imaginative invention in the art of biography. As the "unreliable narrator" emphasizes the fictionality rather than the historical reliability of a narrated story, Carlyle's "unreliable editor" emphasizes the artistic and literary aspect of biography, rather than its claim to be the authentic representation of historical facts.[45]

Thus, unlike *Agnes Grey*, which draws very little attention to itself as an authentically produced document (she does not share original diary entries, for example), and where the novelist uses the form of life writing

primarily as a premise and vehicle for the protagonist's identity formation, *Sartor Resartus* constantly draws attention to its mode of narration
with all of its quirks and flaws. J. Hillis Miller describes the book's
"[calling] attention to itself" as "hyperbolic elaboration"[46] and "rhetorical extravaganc[y]."[47] To put it plainly, the novel is over the top, but, as
Miller continues, "Only a form of writing which constantly destroys itself
and renews itself, as figure follows figure, like phoenix after phoenix in
a constant process of palingenesis, will be true to Carlyle's fundamental
insight, which is 'that all Forms are but Clothes, and temporary.'"[48] Carlyle
presents readers with a highly unconventional work of fiction that boldly
draws our attention to our expectations of how the conventions of documentary evidence and life writing should work.

These are the divergent ways Brontë and Carlyle utilize the affordances
of documentary life writing, and, as Figure 2.2 illustrates, their novels sit
on opposing ends of the spectrum. Importantly, this spectrum does not
measure the *success* of their works or their deployment of these narrative
techniques; rather it emphasizes the significant distance between novels
that both profess to feature authentic narratives of life writing. While the
other subgenres of documentary fiction I cover in this book (epistolary,
adventure, travel, and casebook novels) include a diverse collection of
texts, they tend to share more consistent sets of family traits. Life-writing
novels, however, exhibit tremendous range.

Understanding the Range: *Jane Eyre, David Copperfield,* and *The Memoirs of Barry Lyndon, Esq.*

In order to illuminate the points on this range, I here position a selection of other Victorian novels on the spectrum in order to emphasize the
variety of texts that fit under this category of life-writing documentary
novels and to accentuate how writers creatively exploit the affordances of
this form in differing ways. I by no means cover all relevant works in this
brief survey, but I hope that the examples I give provide clarity on some of
the narrative techniques writers use in this subgenre. Furthermore, having
established the extreme ends of this spectrum, filling in the middle of the
line from *Agnes Grey* to *Sartor Resartus* will underscore the rich variety of
this subgenre of Victorian novels.

The two premier fictional autobiographies of the nineteenth century are Charlotte Brontë's *Jane Eyre* and Charles Dickens's *David Copperfield*. Pennington's monograph on the subgenre covers these novels so extensively that I do not dwell on them long here, but I do highlight the attributes that inform their place on my spectrum (see Figure 2.3). Earlier in this chapter, I cited the "three thematic focuses" of fictional and non-fictional nineteenth-century autobiographies Pennington outlines in her book: an interest in the writer–protagonist's "origins and development, particularly in [their] childhood and education"; "a desire to represent an individual self"; and "a desire for … social recognition of that self's worth and authenticity."[49] *Jane Eyre* and *David Copperfield* certainly map neatly onto this scheme as "coming-of-age stories about realizing an authorial identity."[50] I have placed these novels together to the right of *Agnes Grey* on my spectrum because of how Charlotte Brontë and Dickens more self-consciously explore the reflective point of view of a writer–protagonist. As discussed earlier, although Agnes supposedly writes her own narrative, the documentary premise of the novel largely recedes into the background. *Agnes Grey* undoubtedly shares "thematic focuses" with *Jane Eyre* and *David Copperfield*, but the latter more consistently remind readers that they are engaging with the protagonist's memories and conscientiously constructed life narrative.

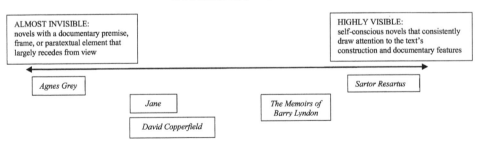

Figure 2.3: Spectrum of life-writing documentary novels: *Agnes Grey*, *Jane Eyre, David Copperfield, The Memoirs of Barry Lyndon, Esq., Sartor Resartus*

Furthermore, the "fictional self-making," as Pennington puts it, of Jane and David instill greater trust in our belief of a stable identity that finds firm establishment within society.[51] In writing about Victorian non-fictional autobiographies, Linda H. Peterson claims these books of life writing "became a Victorian expression of the importance of the individual self."[52] In the case of fictional autobiographies, "Brontë's fiction enabled the construction of a self that could survive and even succeed."[53] Anna Gibson echoes this interpretation in "Charlotte Brontë's First Person," writing that *Jane Eyre* "is the product of a 'person' who has been there from the first, an already-formed self with the authority to shape her story and lead us to the point at which she became the stable self whose voice we have heard all along." Jane "repeatedly steps into her story to remind us there is some*one* writing, and that some*one* is in control of the narrative."[54] In addition to the ways these books reassuringly present a stable identity or the solidi-fying process of the writer–protagonist's individual identity, more often than not "Victorian autobiography derives not only, or even primarily, from a desire to express the self, but also from a belief in the writer's duty to publish a life history for the good of readers, who may profit from both the missteps and the achievements recorded in the autobiographical text."[55] Fictional autobiographies similarly present readers with models of the identity-formation process and their trustworthy life lessons.

This contrasts starkly, of course, with Carlyle's *Sartor Resartus*, in which the very idea of a stable identity is questioned and in which the prospect of fashioning a narrative about an individual is shown to be a fool's errand. Furthermore, while *Jane Eyre* and *David Copperfield* buoy readers' trust in the possibility and value of self-understanding, the Editor of *Sartor Resartus* is left "somewhat exasperated and indeed exhausted" by his work.[56] Despite valiant attempts "to bring what order we can out of this Chaos,"[57] the Editor acknowledges to readers near the end of the narrative that they are likely disappointed and confused, too. He writes,

> [C]an it be hidden from the Editor that many a British Reader sits reading quite bewildered in head, and afflicted rather than instructed by the present Work? Yes, long ago has many a British Reader been, as now, demanding with something like a snarl: Whereto does all this lead; or what use is in it?

In the way of replenishing thy purse, or otherwise aiding they digestive faculty, O British Reader, it leads to nothing, and there is no use in it; but rather the reverse, for it costs thee somewhat."[58]

How this differs from the novels of Brontë and Dickens! The pleasant satisfaction of a confident declaration like "Reader, I married him" is nowhere to be found.[59] *David Copperfield* may culminate with the writer–protagonist's social success, financial stability, and greater self-knowledge and thus inspire readers to follow suit, but *Sartor Resartus* "leads to nothing, and there is no use in it." And, what's more, the Editor claims, the reader does not manage to break even. It has been costly to read the book.

To the right of *Jane Eyre* and *David Copperfield* sits William Makepeace Thackeray's *The Memoirs of Barry Lyndon Esq., of the Kingdom of Ireland* (hereafter referred to as *Barry Lyndon*),[60] a novel that, like *Sartor Resartus*, destabilizes the notion of a fixed and knowable self and consistently draws attention to its fictionality. In *Barry Lyndon*, the memoirist reveals himself to be delusional about his importance and achievements, disrupting readers' trust in him as a narrator and in the possibility of self-knowledge and actualization.

Often described as a picaresque novel, the "memoirs" contain Redmond Barry's reflections on his personal history, starting as a boy in Ireland and continuing with his flight from home as a teenager, time as a soldier in the Seven Years War, work as a spy and escape from the service, gambling partnership with his uncle the Chevalier de Balibari, life-long (and usually nefarious) pursuit of wealth and status, and eventual but inevitable fall from affluence and influence. *Barry Lyndon* shares many characteristics with other Victorian documentary novels discussed in this book: it features a supposed editor who provides footnotes and occasional commentary on Barry's statements, frequent claims of candor and authenticity, and direct addresses to the reader. As the novel's original title suggests, it is also a work of historical fiction. Although Barry is not himself a historical person,[61] the writer–protagonist describes encounters with well-known historical figures and participates in or experiences documented episodes in European history. He supposedly outwits and has drinks with Samuel Johnson, James Boswell, and Oliver Goldsmith; has a cousin who was christened by Jonathan Swift; fights in the Battle of Kunersdorf; and gains 80,000 rubles from Grigory Aleksandrovich Potemkin at the gambling table. While these historical references place Barry in the real world of the eighteenth century, they primarily serve to bolster the writer–protagonist's bombastic claims to greatness.

For what is unique about *Barry Lyndon*, and what informs its place on my proposed spectrum, is its perspective and tone. Barry reveals himself to be an unreliable narrator from the very first page, and Thackeray impressively maintains this stance throughout the novel. In his biography of Thackeray, Anthony Trollope writes, "For an assumed tone of continued irony, maintained through the long memoir of a life, never becoming tedious, never unnatural, astounding us rather by its naturalness, I know nothing equal to *Barry Lyndon*."[62] Unlike *Jane Eyre* and *David Copperfield*, which powerfully and convincingly present trustworthy writer–protagonists on journeys towards self-definition and authority, *Barry Lyndon's* writer–protagonist does not seem to know himself any better at the end of his narrative than at its, and his, beginning. Accordingly, Andrew Sanders notes in his introduction to the Oxford World's Classics edition that "*Barry Lyndon* has vexed readers accustomed to steady, and seemingly trustworthy, narrative voices."[63] Barry, a vain braggart lacking any self-awareness, presents an obviously biased and unapologetic account of his life—a life filled with brash feats of strength, deception, and ruthless exploitation.

Importantly, his entirely warped point of view is clearly evident to the reader in the first few sentences of his book. Barry opens his memoirs:

> Since the days of Adam, there has been hardly a mischief done in this world but a woman has been at the bottom of it. Ever since ours was a family (and that must by very *near* Adam's time,—so old, noble, and illustrious are the Barrys, as everybody knows), women have played a mighty part with the destinies of our race.
>
> I presume that there is no gentleman in Europe that has not heard of the house of Barry of Barryogue, of the kingdom of Ireland, than which a more famous name is not to be found in Gwillim or D'Hozier; and though as a man of the world I have learned to despise heartily the claims of some *pretenders* to high birth who have no more genealogy than the lackey who cleans my

boots, and though I laugh to utter scorn the boasting of many of my countrymen, who are all for descending from kings of Ireland, and talk of a domain no bigger than would feed a pig as if it were a principality; yet truth compels me to assert that my family was the noblest of the island, and, perhaps, of the universal world.[64]

Here Barry makes claims he will repeat throughout his memoirs: that he is perpetually a victim of others (especially women), that he belongs to a great and noble family and is thus entitled to the life of a rich man, and that he presumes others recognize his greatness. While any writer of a memoir or autobiography could be accused of narcissism or at least self-indulgence, Barry's claims are so inflated that readers recognize his narration as bluster from the start. Grandiose phrases like "Since the days of Adam," "so old, noble, and illustrious," and "my family was the noblest of the island, and, perhaps, of the universal world" are outlandish and subjective enough to indicate to readers that "Redmond Barry, Esquire, of Barryville" harbors an overblown view of himself.[65]

Fitz-boodle's fact-checking footnotes also contribute to the reader's understanding of Barry's self-aggrandizing ways. In chapter 7, "Barry leads a garrison life, and finds many friends there," Barry writes of his attempts to exit his service to the Prussian army by ingratiating himself with his captain. "My plan was this," he writes, "I may make myself so necessary to M. de Potzdorff that he will obtain my freedom."[66] Barry discovers, however, that despite his loyal service to Potzdorff, the officer intends to string him along, promising him advancement with no actual ability to promote him beyond his current station. After Barry realizes this, Potzdorff gives him a new assignment, which amazingly places him in the company of his uncle who goes by the elevated title and name, the Chevalier de Balibari, but is actually "Barry, of Ballybarry."[67] Barry informs readers that he has been asked to spy on the Chevalier, but Fitz-boodle interrupts the protagonist to offer a footnote on upcoming events:

The service about which Mr. Barry here speaks has, and we suspect purposely, been described by him in very dubious terms. It is most probable that he was employed to wait at the table of strangers in Berlin, and to bring to the police minister any news concerning them which might at all interest the government. The great Frederick never received a guest without taking these hospitable precautions; and as for the duels which Mr. Barry fights, may we be allowed to hint a doubt as to a great number of these combats? It will be observed, in one or two other parts of his Memoirs, that whenever he is at an awkward pass, or does what the world does not usually consider respectable, a duel in which he is victorious, is sure to ensue; from which he argues that he is a man of undoubted honour.[68]

The supposed editor of these memoirs interjects not only to correct what he thinks is an error in Barry's narrative but also to warn readers about what is ahead and to draw their attention to a pattern of behavior. This means that the footnote both corrects an error and prepares readers for more of them. Thus, even if a reader missed Barry's blatant exaggerations at the beginning of the book, she is now informed by the magazine's editor that the writer of these memoirs is not to be trusted. Robert P. Fletcher writes, "This character/narrator, then, puts us in the awkward position of listening to his story but second-guessing it relentlessly."[69] And there is plenty to second-guess. At various points in his memoirs, Barry brags about his appearance, physical strength and bravery, and great intelligence. He claims to have been "one of the strongest constitutions and finest forms the world ever saw,"[70] argues that "I had an uncommon natural genius for many things, and soon topped in accomplishments most of the persons around me,"[71] and ultimately asks, "Where, in fact, was there a more accomplished gentleman than Redmond de Balibari?"[72]

Because readers know to question or even ignore Barry's claims about himself, Thackeray's novel draws attention, like *Sartor Resartus*, to the fallibility of autobiographical writing and to the constructedness of all identities and narratives. Accordingly, *Barry Lyndon* operates quite differently than *Jane Eyre* or *David Copperfield*, despite all three being retrospective first-person autobiographies. Jane's and David's triumphs illustrate the achievements of self-actualization, while Barry's boasts display the magnitude of his self-deception. A review of the novel published in December of 1856 in the *Saturday Review* comments, "The whole book is founded on the great principle, that if a man only lies hardily enough and long enough, nothing is easier for him than to impose upon himself. In nine cases out of ten, hypocrisy is nothing else than self-deception." The reviewer then adds that *Barry Lyndon* displays "the degree in which a man may bring himself to believe his own lies."[73] Barry has constructed ideas about himself that he has tightly held throughout his life and that he proudly presents to his readers, but our recognition of their detachment from reality creates a rich text that ultimately emphasizes self-creation over self-knowledge. Fletcher accordingly calls *Barry Lyndon* "fiction about fiction-making."[74]

Barry's fiction-making goes beyond exaggerations of accomplishments, however, as he also remakes himself many times in the novel—something that further emphasizes this theme of the malleability of identity. In her article "Legible Liars: Thackeray's *Barry Lyndon* as Professor Imposture," Elizabeth Bleicher writes:

> the threat [Barry] posed for Victorian readers was less his gambling, fraudulence, and social climbing than his insistence on the constructedness and malleability of identity. No other character in 19th-century British literature so persistently embodies the idea that identity is not essential, but is rather a series of accreted iterations of narrative gambits.[75]

One convincing piece of evidence Bleicher provides is a list of the nearly twenty names Barry uses for himself in his memoirs, including Barry of Barryogue, Redmond Barry, Captain Barry, Mr. Redmond, Barry Redmond, Redmond de Balibari, Chevalier Redmond de Balibari, and Barry Lyndon.[76] Unlike David Copperfield and Jane Eyre, whose identities solidify satisfactorily over time, Barry regularly recasts and renames himself in a new role or scheme as he seeks personal, financial, or romantic advancement. What is more, Barry claims that his fabricated identities are no different than the professed pedigrees of his peers. After escaping service to the Prussian military and police, Barry earns considerable wealth with his uncle at gambling tables all over Europe. He describes "a large amethyst signet-ring" he had during this period "and I don't mind confessing that I used to say the jewel had been in my family for several thousand years, having originally belonged to my direct ancestor, his late majesty King Brian Boru, or Barry. I warrant the legends of the Heralds' College are not more authentic than mine was."[77] He admits to lying about this piece of jewelry, an example of his candor in the book, but questions the authenticity of other heirlooms and legends held dearly or proclaimed boldly by the well-to-do and well-connected. He is a liar among liars, so he claims, and as such he does not have to apologize for his embellishment.

In a world like this, what is truth? What is verifiable about a man's life? Barry's comment about the questionable legends of Heralds' College moves us "to infer that this is a world where appearance is generally taken for reality, and where bogus and authentic nobility are pretty much interchangeable."[78] In this world, Barry at the end of his life can refer to himself dying in prison as "the famous and fashionable Barry Lyndon," while the Editor of his memoirs reports that Irish peasants "still entertain the stranger with stories of the daring, and the devilry, and the wickedness, and the fall of Barry Lyndon."[79] He claims fame but the Editor calls him fallen, and this disconnect, steady throughout the novel, playfully undercuts our trust in self-knowledge and actualization. While along with Fitz-Boodle we distinguish Barry's professed self with his actual self, we also recognize that Barry cannot recognize that distinction. He believes himself to be famous and fashionable and is thus not lying at the end of his narrative. He does not lie, but he is wrong—quite wrong. The truth of Barry's life at the end of his memoirs is shown to be quite dependent on one's point of view.

The premise of my spectrum of life-writing documentary novels is that books toward its right end consistently draw attention to the text's construction and documentary features. I have also suggested that the fictional autobiographies of Brontë and Dickens present a comforting view of the individual whereas *Sartor Resartus* questions the possibility of a stable, knowable self. *Barry Lyndon* sits squarely in between these documentary life-writing novels (see Figure 2.3). Thackeray crafts a thoroughly ironic text in which readers both follow Barry's narrative as written and fill in their own sense of events based on what Barry does not say, admit, or recognize. The memoirs' editor regularly draws our attention to the narrative's flaws as a verifiable document, and Barry's obvious and exaggerated construction of himself renders visible the process by which one crafts an understanding of themselves that works to their best advantage.

What is important about these five novels—*Agnes Grey, Jane Eyre, David Copperfield, Barry Lyndon,* and *Sartor Resartus*—is the way they purportedly present the same thing (works of life writing) and yet differ significantly in their messages about society, identity, and the ability of a narrative to capture a human's life. We often default into thinking of Victorian life-writing novels as dominated by the master-narrative of "progress"—the novel of education—but we ignore those texts like *Barry Lyndon* and *Sartor Resartus* that instead of leading towards social integration and identity cohesion advance towards confusion or dissociation. As the Editor writes at the end of *Sartor Resartus,* "We stand in a region of conjectures, where substance has melted into shadow, and one cannot be distinguished from the other."[80]

Here again, then, we have a form that has been called limiting and prehistoric but that actually exhibits tremendous range, and that—perhaps surprisingly—explores key tenets of postmodern ideas. These books have the capacity to reinforce or question notions of identity, and they consciously, and sometimes self-referentially, reflect an awareness that identity is constructed rather than biologically bestowed. Furthermore, this collection of novels may also complicate our usual understanding of what constitutes a realist work when we recognize that *David Copperfield* and *Jane Eyre*—always designated as Victorian realism par excellence—are siblings to a texts like *Barry Lyndon* and *Sartor Resartus* in terms of form.

CHAPTER THREE

Travel and Adventure Novels

Well-Trodden Territory

This book has highlighted the documentary form's narrative constraints in the subgenres of epistolary and life-writing novels. By paying close attention to the constraints inherent in writing narrative fiction entirely by means of documents, we also confront these subgenres' latent potentialities or affordances. As Caroline Levine writes, "With affordances, then, we can begin to grasp the constraints on form that are imposed by materiality itself. One cannot make a poem out of soup or a panopticon out of wool. In this sense, form and materiality are inextricable, and materiality is determinant."[1]

Form and materiality enjoy a well-established bond in travel and adventure fiction. Perhaps more than any other subgenre of Victorian documentary novels, readers associate the adventure tale with the constraining narrative vehicle of the travel journal, memoir, or "discovered" narrative. The titles *Treasure Island* (1883), *Kidnapped* (1886), *Catriona* (1893), *King Solomon's Mines* (1885), and *She: A History of Adventure* (1887) call to mind eyewitness narratives, maps, facsimiles of pottery shards, historical footnotes, and ancient markings on paper, as much as they conjure up shipwrecks, singing pirates, and bagpiping highlanders. These novels bear witness to their journeys, and we tend to remember the materiality of these books as much as their content, their documentary conceits as much as their adventurous plots. Presenting themselves as authentic reports of expeditions, they closely and deliberately mimic their non-fictional counterparts. Accordingly, this chapter first highlights a few popular works of non-fictional Victorian travel writing to reveal the common tropes, narrative strategies, material constraints, and affordances of first-person travel narratives. These include a kind of reluctant posturing by the writer–protagonist and the inclusion of paratextual elements like maps, footnotes, and illustrations. The conventions of Victorian travel writing can seem so compulsory, I argue, that one may believe this form to be quite limiting for writers wanting to craft rich, original prose. A close examination of the novels of Robert Louis Stevenson and H. Rider Haggard, however, discloses that despite this firmly established trait pattern, which I detail in the following section, writers could creatively navigate the subgenre's traditions and utilize its affordances in different ways. Stevenson's *Treasure Island* and *Kidnapped*, in particular, demonstrate what can be achieved with impressive maneuverability within the bounds of a well-established subgenre through tight, nuanced prose that manages to balance the familiar and the strange, the quotidian and the extraordinary. Just as novelists continue to write in the epistolary form, that notoriously confining narrative structure, and exploit its latent potentialities, Stevenson's work indicates that even the most constraining forms afford space for creative manipulation.

Popular Non-Fiction Travel and Adventure Writing

A brief glimpse at the books of Isabella Bird, Mary Seacole, Henry Morton Stanley, and Mary Kingsley reveal the common elements of Victorian travel writing and, consequently, their fake fictional counterparts. Isabella Lucy Bishop, *née* Bird (1831–1904), established herself as an accomplished travel writer in the second half of the nineteenth century. She began traveling internationally as a remedy for poor health in the 1850s, visiting the United States, Canada, and Scotland from her native England. She published her first book of travel writing anonymously in 1856, *The Englishwoman in America*, and it "was accorded fair success."[2] Back in England, after her mother died and her sister settled on the Isle of Mull, Bird decided to seek a better climate and headed out on a journey to New

Zealand, Australia, and Hawaii. Her biographer Pat Barr describes the moment this way:

> In midsummer 1872 a quiet, intelligent-looking dumpy English spinster sailed to Australia in a desperate search for physical and mental health. ... Now she was forty, and added recently to her woes were debilitating attacks of insomnia and nervous prostration. She felt herself growing old, unused, unfulfilled; she was fretful, depressed, frustrated and near mental collapse.[3]

During her trip abroad, she wrote vivid letters to her sister, "to make her younger sister see what she had seen, share what she was doing," and these letters later became her second book—this time published under her name—*The Hawaiian Archipelago: Six Months in the Sandwich Islands* (1875).[4] Bird traveled an extraordinary amount for anyone of her generation, man or woman, and continued writing and publishing. She made journeys to India, Tibet, Turkey, Persia, Kurdistan, Korea, and China, and published nine books of travel narratives and one book of photography. These books contain the hallmark paratextual elements of non-fictional travel writing, including detailed tables of contents, explanatory footnotes, maps, and illustrations. The success of these books can be measured by their multiple printings in London and New York by John Murray and G. P. Putnam respectively. Her book on the Rocky Mountains, for example, went through four editions in just two years. By 1910, six years after Bird's death, Murray published a seventh edition of the book, and it remains in print.[5] Quite significantly, in 1892, she became the first woman named a Fellow of the Royal Geographical Society.

Bird is a compelling figure for a number of reasons. Foremost, of course, is the fact that she traveled great distances and in difficult terrain and conditions when she was in her forties, fifties, and sixties. Barr notes this, titling the third part of her biography "A Lady's Life on the Back of Yak, Pony, Mule, Stallion; In Junk, Wupan, Steamer, Sampan; In Stable, Tent, Hut, Caravanserai; Across the Deserts, Over the Plains and Up the Mountains."[6] Her means of travel and sites of interest were varied. When Bird was in her early sixties, she traveled through Korea, "explored the Han River and crossed the Diamond mountains to the east coast of the peninsula. After a visit to Chinese Manchuria she went up the Yangtze (Yangzi), through Szechwan (Sichuan), to the Tibetan border, spending fifteen months and travelling 8000 miles in China alone."[7] And that was just one of many expeditions.

Besides the remarkable nature of her taxing journeys, Bird is noteworthy for her skill as a writer. One review of her bestselling *A Lady's Life in the Rocky Mountains* (1879) published in the *Spectator* claimed that it was "of more interest than most of the novels which it has been our lot to encounter, and in fact comprises character, situation and dramatic effect enough to make ninety-nine novels out of a hundred look pallid and flat in comparison."[8] Her descriptions of Estes Park are quite captivating. She writes,

> Here and there the lawns are so smooth, the trees so artistically grouped, a lake makes such an artistic foreground, or a water-fall comes tumbling down with such an apparent feeling for the picturesque, that I am almost angry with Nature for her close imitation of art. But in another hundred yards Nature, glorious, unapproachable, inimitable, is herself again, raising one's thoughts reverently upwards to her Creator and ours. Grandeur and sublimity not softness, are the features of Estes Park.[9]

Drawn into Bird's descriptions of natural beauty and charmed by her self-deprecations, the reviewer in *The Examiner* praised her in similarly grand terms: "Miss Bird's modest little volume appears like an oasis in a desert of print. ... The professional author could have made a bigger volume out of the wealth of experiences which Miss Bird has passed through; but it would be difficult to have made a more satisfactory one."[10] Particularly impressive about this review is the fact that it follows two others under the heading "Books of Travel." The first publication discussed, *Travel and Trout in the Antipodes: An Angler's Sketches in Tasmania and New Zealand*, by William Senior, gets a generally positive, although overall lukewarm review. The second, *The Ascent of the Matterhorn*, by Edward Whymper, gets annihilated as "mainly the abridgment of an old book published eight years ago," "over-familiar," and containing the ascent of a peak that "has been ascended at least 159 times—once or twice, we understand, by ladies—which proves that its scaling is by no means so difficult."

The reviewer admits that Whymper's story, although full of "egotism," is well told and contains "exquisite" illustrations, but even those images fail because the

> subjects chosen are … in many cases, bad in the extreme, being illustrative of nothing save a nearly impossible incident, or some not overmodestly related "adventure." Nor are they all equally good. For instance, nothing could be finer as an engraving, or in worse taste as an illustration, than that facing p.78, while the scene opposite p.120 is a useful illustration, but a poor bit of art.[11]

In short, the components that make a compelling travel narrative are missing in Whymper's book. He has an adventurous story, but it is old news; he has professional-quality illustrations, but they fit the material poorly; he has maps, including one in color, but the terrain displayed has already been traversed by over a hundred others, including some women.[12] To return to Levine's language of potentialities, Whymper's *Ascent of the Matterhorn* fails to take advantage of the affordances of the form. He has the basis for a successful book, but his execution fails in his deployment of the travel narrative's various textual and visual components.

Bird's book by contrast, slim though it may be, is an "an oasis in a desert of print," and this is despite the fact that she faced a similar challenge to Whymper. As the reviewer writes, "Since the Rocky Mountains and the great West have been vulgarized by the Pacific Railroad, the Press has poured out shelf-fuls of silly superficial tourist impressions, hardly one of which was worthy of serious notice."[13] In other words, like Whymper, Bird writes about a subject many others have already described, and yet her "informal letters" capture "more" and are "infinitely better."[14] Importantly for this study, the *Spectator* reviewer credits Bird's use of "character, situation and dramatic effect" in making her book "of more interest" than many novels.[15] This comment not only praises Bird's storytelling ability, but it also reveals how fiction and non-fiction writers work from the same toolkit. As Carl Thompson writes in *Travel Writing*,

> Even in a form with the apparent immediacy of a travel journal or diary, a writer necessarily picks out significant recent events,

and organises those events, and his or her reflections on them, into some sort of narrative, however brief. Travel *experience* is thus crafted into travel *text*, and this crafting process must inevitably introduce into the text, to a greater or lesser degree, a fictive dimension.[16]

Susan Bassnett calls this transformation from experiences into publishable narrative a "fictionalizing process."[17] As she and Thompson suggest, this process is not necessarily an act of deception; rather, it is a means of making human experiences understandable, readable, and compelling. Writing in 1884, Stevenson argued, "The art of narrative, in fact, is the same, whether it is applied to the selection and illustration of a real series of events or of an imaginary series."[18] His comment conveys why we use the term *creative non-fiction* today.

The reviewer of Bird's book makes clear that readers enjoy novelistic elements in travel narratives and that they judge novels harshly when non-fiction makes better use of characterization and plotting. Furthermore, the reviewer articulates how Bird maximized the affordances of a travel book. Unlike Whymper, who squandered that opportunity in his *Ascent of the Matterhorn*, Bird took advantage of the form's inherent potentialities, including those essential to fictional storytelling listed previously, as well as those seen as standard in non-fictional travel writing, like the inclusion of a detailed table of contents and illustrations. An examination of Bird's writing, especially her early books, provides a sense of the range of affordances available to writers working in this genre and in travel and adventure fiction of the Victorian period.

The prefatory material of Bird's books reveals much about her approach to this form and her way of positioning herself as a writer. Like many travel narratives, her books open with prefaces that explain the texts' origins. Her opening remarks typically take the same tone and, despite the varying geographical regions in which she traveled, communicate generally the same thing: she presents herself as an eager traveler but reluctant author. In her earliest books she expresses this reluctance by apologizing for the unpolished nature of her writing. *The Hawaiian Archipelago* begins with a dedication to Bird's sister "to whom these letters were originally written." This brief note already prompts readers to see her writing as intimate, immediate, and authentic. As letters to a dear sister, readers expect them to contain personal details fitting an intimate relationship, to feature the writer's thoughts in the immediate aftermath of each day's journeys, and to consist of authentic reports of her experiences that she wants to share with her sister, not a reading public. She writes a couple pages later in her Preface,

> The letters which follow were written to a near relation, and often hastily and under great difficulties of circumstance, but even with these and other disadvantages, they appear to me the best form of conveying my impressions in their original vividness. With the exception of certain omissions and abridgments, they are printed as they were written, and for such demerits as arise from this mode of publication, I ask the kind indulgence of my readers.[19]

This apologetic explanation of the book's origins allows Bird to distance herself from criticism that her writing is too informal or inaccurate. The flaws her letters may contain only boost her credibility as an amateur writer sending letters to her sister—something common and relatable enough.

She strategically pairs this apologetic tone with an expressed reluctance to publish her letters, which further enhances her credibility as an eyewitness. She did not set out to publish a travel book; rather, she had gone "travelling for health" in the Hawaiian islands, and

> At the close of my visit, my Hawaiian friends urged me strongly to publish my impressions and experiences, on the ground that the best books already existing, besides being old, treat chiefly of aboriginal customs and habits now extinct, and of the introduction of Christianity and subsequent historical events. They also represented that I had seen the islands more thoroughly than any foreign visitor … My friends at home, who were interested in my narratives, urged me to give them to a wider circle, and my inclinations led me in the same direction, with a longing to make others share something of my own interest and enjoyment.[20]

Bird claims that her friends at home and abroad "urged" her publish; it was not her idea or original intention, and this helps bolster her against criticism that she writes purely from self-interest. One could argue that this posture of the apologetic and reluctant writer is necessitated by Bird's gender: it advantages her to present herself as a humble writer of sisterly letters rather than a rough-and-tumble traveler, although ultimately that is what her books reveal.

The prefatory material of all her travel books strike this tone and make similar claims of apology regarding the form, immediacy, and intimate nature of the included correspondence. What is striking about this is that following her successful publication of *The Hawaiian Archipelago* she had an established audience. It is a bit odd that in the "Prefatory Note" of her following book, *A Lady's Life in the Rocky Mountains*, she states, "These letters, as their style sufficiently indicates, were written without the remotest idea of publication."[21] Can that be? As she did in her previous book, she presents herself as one who consented to publish her writing "at the request" of another—this time the editor of *Leisure Hour*. Her posture of humility and passivity may enhance her credibility, but this posture belies her actual writing process of intentionally shaping material for readers. Barr writes that Bird's

> long, discursive, personal, discerning epistles were written more or less on the spot like war-reports and then sent to Hennie, who shared their contents with a small circle of intimate women friends. On returning home, it was Isabella's habit to "excise a mass of personal detail" from the letters, edit them, add chunks of historical and political information and then publish them in book form.[22]

These apologies and explanations at the beginning of Bird's books are a convention of travel writing, an affordance, that Bird uses to her advantage. Proof of this lies in the fact that she continued making these statements even after she achieved renown as a travel writer. One would think that she could stop apologizing for her style of writing after the success of her books; she no longer needs to act as though she lacks experience. But the posture of a credible eyewitness, innocently conveying experiences to readers, without the corrupting influence of writing for the public and in a form that can be forgiven for minor mistakes given the extremities of the environment in which they were written, benefits her significantly. It gives her flexibility. She can write her "war-reports," as Barr describes them, on the spot, jotting down her thoughts in vivid prose, but then she can also go back to them later, and while keeping the immediacy of the original letters she can amend them in order to engage and inform readers as best she can. She presents herself as being an authority as well as a significantly constrained correspondent, and this posture and balancing act affords her great latitude in representing her experiences.

Mary Seacole, another Victorian travel writer, carefully negotiated her posture on the page in some similar ways. Seacole was born in 1805 to a Scottish father and Jamaican Creole mother in Kingston, Jamaica. The details of her early life are few, but she acquired skill and experience in nursing and eventually embarked on an entirely self-driven mission to serve British soldiers in the Crimean War. Her *Wonderful Adventures of Mrs. Seacole in Many Lands* "edited by W. J. S.," was published in 1857 and met with immediate success. She presents herself with more confidence than Bird does in her books, but Seacole nonetheless emphasizes the innocence of her passion for nursing and requests the forgiveness of her readers on various occasions. These requests and other rhetorical moves help temper her confidence and give readers the sense that, despite her bold claims and actions, she is also capable of sincere humility and commendable labor. She is, in short, a trustworthy reporter.

A close reading of her book's opening paragraph reveals Seacole's careful posturing as a respectable and authentic conveyor of these "wonderful adventures." She opens her narrative:

> I was born in the town of Kingston, in the island of Jamaica, some time in the present century. As a female, and a widow, I may be well excused giving the precise date of this important event. But I do not mind confessing that the century and myself were both young together, and that we have grown side by side into age and consequence. I am a Creole, and have good Scotch blood coursing in my veins. My father was a soldier, of an old Scotch family; and to him I often trace my affection for a camp-life, and

my sympathy with what I have heard my friends call "the pomp, pride, and circumstance of glorious war." Many people have also traced to my Scotch blood that energy and activity which are not always found in the Creole race, and which have carried me to so many varied scenes: and perhaps they are right. I have often heard the term "lazy Creole" applied to my country people; but I am sure I do not know what it is to be indolent. All my life long I have followed the impulse which led me to be up and doing; and so far from resting idle anywhere, I have never wanted inclination to rove, nor will powerful enough to find a way to carry out my wishes. That these qualities have led me into many countries, and brought me into some strange and amusing adventures, the reader, if he or she has the patience to get through this book, will see. Some people, indeed, have called me quite a female Ulysses. I believe that they intended it as a compliment; but from my experience of the Greeks, I do not consider it a very flattering one.[23]

Seacole follows her straightforward opening sentence with apologetic phrases like "I may be well excused" and "I do not mind confessing," as she politely avoids providing readers her age.[24] Here, and throughout the paragraph, she presents herself as a natural and neutral human being rather than a bold, entrepreneurial risk-taker. She and "the century ... were both young together" and "have grown side by side," a description that emphasizes inevitability and ordinary development. Perhaps establishing this kind of natural neutrality is important before she goes on to describe her ethnicity. Angelica Poon writes that Seacole "begins her narrative by carefully plotting out the co-ordinates of her personal history and providing her readers with the racial compass with which she would like them to navigate the rest of her story."[25] Aware she has a majority-white audience, Seacole lays claim to her "Scotch blood" and credits her father's occupation as a soldier for getting her interested in military life. Following this statement, however, she pushes back against the racist notion that her good qualities come from her white father only—the idea that because Creoles are typically "indolent," her work ethic must come from her Scotch blood. She assures readers they will see the error in this view for themselves, a rhetorical move that again communicates a sense of naturalness to her narrative. She does not have to prove the inaccuracy of this racist idea to her readers; they will see it themselves naturally as they read. Her opening paragraph thus establishes a posture of a frank yet polite writer who wants readers to trust and respect her.[26]

Bird and Seacole built impressive reputations as accomplished travelers and writers, but probably the most well-known work of Victorian travel writing is Henry Morton Stanley's *How I Found Livingstone*. From the time of its publication in 1872 up to 1900, there were eighteen editions of the book published in England and the United States.[27] The book traces the expedition tasked with locating the explorer and missionary David Livingstone. *How I Found Livingstone* was widely mocked when published. Florence Nightingale said it was "the very worst book on the very best subject I ever saw in my life"[28]—but it ultimately enjoyed great success. Like other works of Victorian travel writing, it contains personal narrative, illustrations, and a map. It also begins with the requisite explanation of the journey's origins and premise of the book. Any reader will recognize Stanley's opening chapter as particularly dramatic:

> On the sixteenth day of October, in the year of our Lord one thousand eight hundred and sixty-nine, I am in Madrid, fresh from the carnage at Valencia. At 10 A.M. Jacopo, at No.— Calle de la Cruz, handed me a telegram: on opening I find it reads, "Come to Paris on important business." The telegram is from Jas. Gordon Bennett, jun., the young manager of the "New York Herald."
>
> Down came my pictures from the walls of my apartments on the second floor; into my trunks go my books and souvenirs, my clothes are hastily collected, some half washed, some from the clothes-line half dry, and after a couple of hours of hasty hard work my portmanteaus are strapped up, and labelled for "Paris."[29]

His invocation of "the year of our Lord" in the first sentence heightens the import of what follows, even if cheaply, and is followed by a series of actions that occur to the author. Like Bird, he is passive: he is "in Madrid," is "handed ... a telegram," and "Down" come the pictures and the clothes into his suitcase, which "are hastily collected" and "strapped up, and labelled." The adventure has found Stanley; he merely accepts the call.

Stanley's explanation at the beginning of his book remains in keeping with Bird's posturing in her work. He certainly does not come off as humble, in the slightest, but Stanley does present himself as one directed to act rather than one who seeks out the action. For example, Stanley expresses surprise at being asked to look for the famous explorer,

> "What!" said I, "do you really think I can find Dr. Livingstone? Do you mean me to go to Central Africa?"
>
> "Yes; I mean that you shall go, and find him wherever you may hear that he is, and to get what news you can of him, and perhaps"—delivering himself thoughtfully and deliberately— "the old man may be in want:—take enough with you to help him should he require it. Of course you will act according to your own plans, and do what you think best—BUT FIND LIVINGSTONE!"[30]

This exchange reads much more like the beginning of a Haggard novel than a somber rescue mission and journalistic endeavor, but the veracity of this moment means little when we consider the importance of this kind of gesture in Victorian travel writing. Like Bird, Stanley must explain the impetus for his journey, show some reluctance or surprise at being sent out, and establish reader expectations for what they will find in the pages to come. Bird instructs her readers that what they will find are mere letters with the flaws inherent in that form. Stanley informs his readers that he has been tasked with one mission above all others—"FIND LIVING-STONE!"—but has also been given the freedom "to act according to [his] own plans." Readers expect, then, that the narrative will drive towards the discovery of the lost explorer but will likely contain some wanderings as well. Bird presents herself as an amateur writer and thus positions herself to be forgiven for flaws in her descriptions, and Stanley presents himself as driven toward a specified end as well as accorded the freedom to change course as needed. For both, this self-positioning in the prefatory material of their books affords them some flexibility in terms of content, style, and pacing and is designed as a kind of defense mechanism against criticism.

Mary Kingsley (1862–1900), another successful Victorian travel writer, begins her bestselling *Travels in West Africa* (1897) similarly by opening her book with an apology. She writes in her book's preface, "To

THE READER.—What this book wants is not a simple Preface but an apology, and a very brilliant and convincing one at that."[31] This posturing contrasts starkly with Stanley's bombastic opening, but like him and Bird she must explain the origins of the work and set her readers' expectations and claim authenticity despite her flaws. Like Stanley, she recognizes the role of her publisher in bringing the book to fruition, saying,

> I cannot forbear from mentioning my gratitude to Mr. George Macmillan for his patience and kindness with me,—a mere jungle of information on West Africa. Whether you my reader will share my gratitude is, I fear, doubtful, for if it had not been for him I should never have attempted to write a book at all, and in order to excuse his having induced me to try I beg to state that I have written only on things that I know from personal experience and very careful observation.[32]

In the book's preface, she apologizes, excuses, and begs, positioning herself as a reluctant author who nonetheless has done her best to record authentic experiences drawn from "very careful observation." This posture of inexperienced and yet honest writer allows Kingsley the freedom to write from her own perspective while also defending against claims of inaccuracy and ignorance.

These examples from Bird, Seacole, Stanley, and Kingsley show how firmly established this kind of posturing was in Victorian travel writing. The stance of the honest writer composing authentic documents and using "character, situation and dramatic effect" to write about a real journey works wonderfully to capture the interest of readers when balanced with paratextual elements like maps and illustrations.[33] The consistent application of these conventions suggests how useful writers found them when narrativizing the sometimes disorienting experiences of an expedition. Of course, all genres have their own sets of norms and common traits, but one inherent risk with a decidedly fixed genre like travel writing is that its books will become too predictable. The standards become so entrenched in terms of stance, content, and form that readers will find the material stale and lose interest. Whymper's *The Ascent of the Matterhorn* failed to avoid this risk and prompted a reviewer to call the book "over-familiar."[34]

Novels that mimic non-fictional travel writing also feature these conventions and carry this risk. Novelists aim to use "character, situation and dramatic effect" successfully, craft a reliable eyewitness, and employ paratextual elements like maps, illustrations, and footnotes that verify elements of the trip. The posture of the honest and reluctant reporter, the content of a transformational journey, and the form of letters, journal entries or memoirs all carry over into travel and adventure documentary novels from their non-fictional cousins.

Fictional Travel and Adventure Novels: Stevenson, Haggard, and Ragged

These conventions of non-fictional travel and adventure writing do not carry over ambiguously into the realm of fiction. H. Rider Haggard's novel *She: A History of Adventure* contains a supposed facsimile of an ancient sherd, an editorial introduction that includes a corroborating letter, the manuscript of "a real African adventure," and footnotes that provide historical or editorial context to material in the main text.[35] *King Solomon's Mines* begins with a dedication from the writer–protagonist pledging that the book is a "faithful but unpretending record of a remarkable adventure" and includes the "sketch map" that guides the travelers through "Kukuanaland."[36] Ken Gelder writes that

> with popular fiction, generic identities are *always* visible. …
> Popular fiction announces those identities loudly and unambiguously: you know and need to know immediately that this
> is romance, or a work of crime fiction (and/or spy fiction), or
> science fiction, or fantasy, or horror, or a western, or an historical
> popular novel or an adventure novel.[37]

The visibility of genre-markers, guide and calibrate reader expectations and identify the book as part of an ongoing tradition. In the case of travel writing, the posturing of the writer–protagonist and the presence of corroborating evidence serve frequently as these markers.

When working in a well-established tradition like this, the novelist may lean heavily on the customary tropes, character types, morals, and forms of previously published books, and such fixity of content and form can impede a writer trying to do something novel. The documentary novels of Stevenson, however, show us how a writer can innovate within the constraints of a firmly fixed form. Like Bird, who was able to craft a compelling travel narrative of her journey through the Rocky Mountains despite the fact that there already were "shelf-fuls of silly superficial tourist impressions" published on the subject, Stevenson maneuvers the established conventions of travel writing without resorting to boilerplate openings, overworked plots, and character types. Stevenson's writing thus displays elasticity in travel and adventure writing despite the fixity of its conventions, the constraints of the documentary form, and the risk of cheap mimicry.

Perhaps "*mimicry*" is too generous and academic a word since Stevenson himself termed *Treasure Island* a work of "*plagiarism*." In a piece he published in 1894, titled "My First Book," he wrote,

> No doubt the parrot once belonged to Robinson Crusoe. No doubt the skeleton is conveyed from Poe. ... The stockade, I am told, is from *Masterman Ready.* ... It is my debt to Washington Irving that exercises my conscience, and justly so, for I believe plagiarism was rarely carried farther. ... Billy Bones, his chest, the company in the parlour, the whole inner spirit, and a good deal of the material detail of my first chapters—all were there, all were the property of Washington Irving.[38]

Stevenson admits to stealing elements of the novel's content from other works of adventure fiction, but he also mimics earlier works of non-fictional travel writing in *Treasure Island*, using a documentary form with a writer–protagonist who is encouraged to share his story not unlike a "real" adventurer going out and reporting her experiences afterwards in a published memoir.[39]

Of course, Stevenson wrote non-fictional travel books himself. Like Bird, Stevenson traveled to ease his poor health, and his first three books, published in close succession, were works of travel writing: *An Inland Voyage* (1878), *Edinburgh: Picturesque Notes* (1878), and *Travels with a Donkey in the Cévennes* (1879). Two of these, *An Inland Voyage* and

Travels with a Donkey, contain prefatory material akin to Bird, Seacole, Stanley, and Kingsley, and are indicative of his growing skill as a writer to work within and experiment beyond conventions. His preface to *An Inland Voyage* hits the requisite notes of the humble, reluctant writer while also making light of this traditional posturing. He begins,

> To equip so small a book with a preface is, I am half afraid, to sin against proportion. But a preface is more than an author can resist, for it is the reward of his labours. When the foundation stone is laid, the architect appears with his plans, and struts for an hour before the public eye. So with the writer in his preface: he may have never a word to say, but he must show himself for a moment in the portico, hat in hand, and with an urbane demeanour.[40]

Stevenson claims this introductory material to be required of an author and an award for the labor of writing, but his description of the author's duty also mocks this kind of performance. He recognizes the mixture of humility and vanity that typify these prefaces as he emphasizes that his book is too "small" to need one and yet describes the way the "architect appears ... and *struts* ... before the public eye" (emphasis added). In the following paragraph, Stevenson makes this claim directly: "It is best, in such circumstances, to represent a delicate shade of manner between humility and superiority: as if the book had been written by some one else, and you had merely run over it and inserted what was good."[41] The balance of humility and superiority Stevenson describes fits neatly with the prefaces earlier cited from Bird's books: the writer expressing humility while also establishing some authority over the subject matter. Stevenson's acquaintance with and use of this posture, though, also incorporates a level of humor that Bird's does not as he draws our attention to the oddity of an author acting as though "the book had been written by some one else." Stevenson ends up calling the preface "no more than an advertisement for readers," and this is something he carries forward into his next books along with his sense of humor at the convention.[42]

In *Travels with a Donkey* he opts for a letter to his friend Sidney Colvin to serve as the book's preface and dedication. He does not describe the premise of the book or his authority in writing it, but he does establish intimacy with his readers through this endearing note in which he writes, "Every book is, in an intimate sense, a circular letter to the friends of him who writes it. They alone take his meaning; they find private messages, assurances of love, and expressions of gratitude dropped for them in every corner. The public is but a generous patron who defrays the postage."[43] While Stevenson makes this statement in order to dedicate the book to someone in his private circle of friends, the opening message also subtly informs the reader that she will find private meanings, messages, assurances, and expressions in these pages. He uses similar subtlety in addressing this sticky issue of writing for the public. Whereas Bird shuns the idea of writing for a public audience in her books (even when it is clear that she carefully prepared her writing for public consumption), Stevenson situates the reader as a "generous patron who defrays the postage" of a private letter. Designating readers as conduits to communicating with dear friends enhances Stevenson's posture of intimacy and humility. He has not sought out readers so that his journey can be advertised far and wide; rather, he has sought out readers, or so he says, to cover the cost of sending a private letter. Although Stevenson's prefatory letter contains more subtle artistry than Bird's, Stanley's, or Kingsley's, his stance is essentially the same: Reader, here in this book you will find genuine reports of experiences that are more personal than public.

Stevenson's ability to address the issues of authenticity and public writing without the false modesty, bombast, or overwrought nervousness of Bird, Stanley, or Kingsley reveals not only his talent but also the surprising range of these conventions of travel writing. Stevenson demonstrates that a writer can begin with this kind of posturing without resorting to a flat, boilerplate opening. His continued use of these conventions of travel and adventure writing also indicates, in part, their cultural durability. A writer of his talent, one could imagine, might dispose of these constraining generic conventions altogether, but Stevenson recognized their potential if used in combination with compelling, psychologically subtle and tight prose.

He strikes this balance wonderfully in *Treasure Island*. The novel was initially serialized in the boys' magazine *Young Folks* from October 1881 to the end of January 1882, and was attributed to Captain George North, an attribution that certainly lent the tale some legitimacy in a publication aimed at young readers. It also contributed to the façade of a sea captain serving as courier of Jim Hawkins's eyewitness account. Stevenson dropped this pseudonym when he revised *Treasure Island* to be published in book form by Cassell & Company in 1883, but he retained the posture of a true story in Jim's first-person narrative, added an opening poem titled "To the Hesitating Purchaser," and put in a map that is presented as the facsimile of an authentic document from the novel.[44]

The opening poem does what Stevenson writes in *An Inland Voyage* a preface should do: it serves as an advertisement for readers. Facing the book's table of contents, "To the Hesitating Purchaser" reads:

> If sailor tales to sailor tunes,
>   Storm and adventure, heat and cold,
> If schooners, islands, and maroons
>   And Buccaneers and buried Gold,
> And all the old romance, retold
>   Exactly in the ancient way,
> Can please, as me they pleased of old,
>   The wiser youngsters of to-day:
>
> —So be it, and fall on! If not,
>   If studious youth no longer crave,
> His ancient appetites forgot,
>   Kingston, or Ballantyne the brave,
> Or Cooper of the wood and wave:
>   So be it, also! And may I
> And all my pirates share the grave
>   Where these and their creations lie![45]

This poem informs the potential buyer of the book's subject matter while also establishing the novel's place in a line of adventurous tales, connecting *Treasure Island* to the works of W. H. G. Kingston, R. M. Ballantyne, and James Fenimore Cooper. The poem clearly echoes the preface of Ballantyne's *The Coral Island* (1858), in which he writes in the voice of Ralph

Rover, the narrator of the novel: "If there is any boy or man who loves to be melancholy and morose, and who cannot enter with kindly sympathy into the regions of fun, let me seriously advise him to shut my book and put it away. It is not meant for him."[46] Stevenson's bit of verse carries on this kind of warning to unimaginative readers while also pointing to the enduring conventions of travel and adventure writing. Like Bird, he offers an apology for his book's style, claiming that this book is like others in terms of content and form, like "all the old romance, retold/Exactly in the ancient way." The poem thus pays homage to some of Stevenson's favorites while also suggesting that the writer believes in the value of "the ancient way."

This "ancient way" includes the use of a first-person, document-based narrative, accompanied by proofs of the journey—a norm, as we have seen, of both non-fictional and fictional travel writing. To return to the affordances of travel writing exalted by the reviewer of Bird's *A Lady's Life in the Rocky Mountains*, when well done, these books have the capacity effectively to pair images with text and to utilize "character, situation and dramatic effect." Stevenson powerfully pairs image with text in *Treasure Island*'s opening pages by including Captain Flint's map, the document that becomes part of a deadly search in the novel. Unlike some maps that merely display the path of a completed or intended journey, the map of *Treasure Island* has elements that push it beyond the mere status of bonus material. The map supposedly contains the markings of multiple characters: Captain Flint, Billy Bones, and Jim Hawkins.[47] The map's apparent authenticity comes in part from these markings, which suggest that the map has been used in the manner described in the book. As Sally Bushell points out,

> In modern editions of *Treasure Island*, the map is usually reproduced in black and white. ... In the first-edition map, however, different handwritings are distinguished by ink color: Flint's comments are in red, Billy Bones's in brown, and Jim's in blue. These different colors draw attention to the fact that annotations to the map are given in three distinct hands, each representative of their authors.[48]

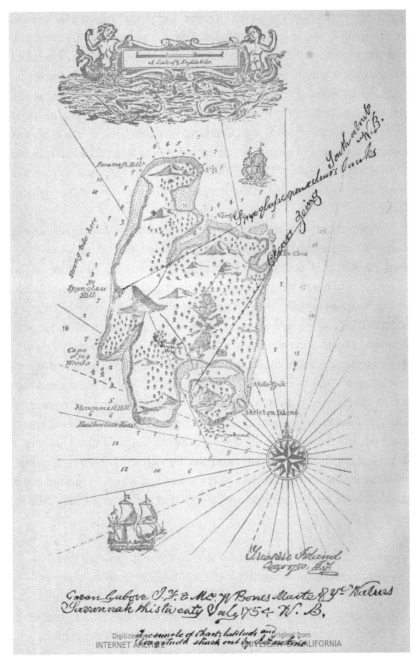

Figure 3.1: Map of Treasure Island. *Treasure Island.* London, Paris, & New York: Cassell & Company, 1883. University of California Libraries

The different ink colors also contribute to the map's perceived intimacy with the narrative. When the colors are reduced to the black and white of a photocopy, the map loses some of its power as it becomes more distanced from the original and the supposed inks of Flint, Bones, and Hawkins. Additionally, the original color map captures Stevenson's choice to present it as supposedly authentic proof of the journey (Figure 3.1).

The map is also part of a larger established apparatus of travel writing in which writers seek ways to visually represent the scope, treacherousness, and plausibility of a journey. In the case of *Treasure Island*, the map is not merely bonus paratextual material included in the book's endpapers; the map is an important object in the novel. In "Paratext or Imagetext? Interpreting the Fictional Map," Bushell claims that fictional maps included in a book's endpapers, like that of *Treasure Island*, are "likely to involve a strong design element intended to have an aesthetic appeal," but that overemphasizing "design in an endpaper map misleadingly encourages the reader to respond to it as primarily illustrative or decorative and thus serves to devalue its integrative meaning."[49] The map of *Treasure Island*, in fact, is not particularly useful in illustrating where the action of the book takes place as we cannot determine where this island actually is or if it has a real-world referent. In other words, for readers, it is not particularly helpful as a guide of how and where to travel. Instead, the map, with its markings by Flint, Bones, and Hawkins, serves multiple purposes: it illustrates the treasure's pull on different men to discover its location, it incites action in the book at various moments and so is central to the novel's plot, it works as a lure on the reader, it is a cognitive link between readers and characters who puzzle over the map's markings and debate its value, and it is an article of accomplishment and destruction all at once. Jim says near the end of the novel that the pull of Flint's treasure ultimately claims "the lives of seventeen men from the *Hispaniola*. How many it had cost in the amassing, what blood and sorrow, what good ships scuttled on the deep, what brave men walking the plank blindfold, what shot of cannon, what shame and lies and cruelty, perhaps no man alive could tell."[50] In this manner, as Bushell describes, "fictional maps are not mere appendages to these texts but rather form a vital, integrated part of their meaning."[51] The map of *Treasure Island*, like Stevenson's novel as a whole, meets conventional expectations while also maximizing their possibilities, going beyond a simple illustration to a multimodal object that serves as plot device, documentary evidence, and thematic artifact. Thus, while we have considered the documentary form as particularly constraining on authors, Stevenson exhibits an extraordinary ability to impart layers of meaning into seemingly simple genre conventions.

Stevenson employs similar introductory, paratextual elements in *Kidnapped*. Like *Treasure Island* before it, *Kidnapped* was initially serialized in *Young Folks*, from May to the end of July 1886 and then published in a single volume by Cassell & Company.[52] And, like *Treasure Island*, the first edition includes a color map. It is not a replica of an object from the narrative; rather, it is the "Sketch of the cruise of the brig Covenant and the probable course of David Balfour's wanderings." In this way, the map of *Kidnapped* seems a bit more distanced from the action of the novel than Flint's marked-up chart in *Treasure Island*. It is not a coveted material object that spurs action in the text, or a spatial guide used by the protagonist, but instead is a document created after the journey's completion to situate David's travels for the benefit of readers. Even when a map is mentioned by David in the narrative itself, at the beginning of chapter 12, he writes, "And here I must explain; and the reader would do well to look at a map."[53] David goes on to describe the path taken by the brig and reveals that "the captain had no chart" so "he preferred to go by west of Tiree and come up under the southern coast of the great Isle of Mull."[54] The map, then, is entirely for the benefit of readers, since the characters in the text do not have one themselves. The map, along with the narrative, works to embed David's journey in real, recognizable places. In *Treasure Island*, although the map is presented as genuine and has markings which vouch for its authenticity, the map cannot be used by readers in any practical way. They cannot make their way to Treasure Island by using the map. In *Kidnapped*, on the other hand, Stevenson does the opposite, employing the map to further ground his novel historically and geographically. Certainly this fits with *Kidnapped*'s status as a work of historical as well as documentary fiction. David travels to real places, interacts with historical figures, and witnesses a historical event, the Appin murder. The map underscores this schema as it highlights the geographical terrain, distance, and circuity of David's "Wanderings." The map's label as "the probable course" of David's adventure reflects a kind of editorial honesty, as if the map's creator has done his best to put on paper an approximation of so extraordinary a tale.

In addition to the map, Stevenson overtly marks *Kidnapped* as a work of memoir. He borrows directly from Defoe in labeling *Kidnapped* for his readers both on the book's title page and at the beginning of the first chapter. The full title, echoing *Robinson Crusoe*, reads,

> Kidnapped: Being Memoirs of the Adventures of David Balfour in the Year 1751: How he was Kidnapped and Cast away; his Sufferings in a Desert Isle; his Journey in the Wild Highlands; his acquaintance with Alan Breck Stewart and other notorious Highland Jacobites; with all that he Suffered at the hands of his Uncle, Ebenezer Balfour of Shaws, falsely so-called: Written by Himself, and now set forth by ROBERT LOUIS STEVENSON.[55]

The posture of authenticity Stevenson depicts in *Kidnapped* differs from other non-fictional travel books in that the book's supposed author, David Balfour, does not present himself as a reluctant writer. Rather, *Kidnapped*'s veil of authenticity comes in its presentation of concrete details about the journey up front, the path outlined on the map, the important events enumerated on the title page, the specificity of 1751, the careful mimicry of eighteenth-century paratextual elements, and, of course, his detailed prose, complete with dialogue in Scots.

Stevenson artfully integrates these paratextual elements with first-person, eyewitness accounts that like many other works of travel writing provide a sense of intimacy and immediacy, despite their reflective, after-the-fact stance. Again, Stevenson shows himself able to exploit the affordances of this subgenre of documentary fiction despite the limitations inherent in a first-person narrative. Tom Sleigh, the award-winning poet, is featured on a *New Yorker* poetry podcast in 2017 discussing a Seamus Heaney poem called "In the Attic," which references *Treasure Island*. During the interview, Sleigh offers a description of what makes Stevenson's rendering of Jim's adventure in *Treasure Island* so remarkable. He says, "For me it's that kind of limpid, no-sweat English prose in which everything is registered descriptively with perfect accuracy and in a syntax that you feel absolutely tracks the speaker's consciousness as they're perceiving things."⁵⁶ Sleigh's praise of Stevenson's style draws our attention to its realistic qualities, despite the fact that Stevenson is often dismissed as a writer of romance. Furthermore, Sleigh's sense that the prose in *Treasure Island* "absolutely tracks the speaker's consciousness" speaks to an immediacy inherent in Jim's narrative despite the fact that he is supposedly recalling all of these events out of his past.

Jim proves himself to be a competent storyteller, but he claims reluctance at the beginning of the narrative, in keeping with so many other works of Victorian travel writing. He begins,

> Squire Trelawney, Dr. Livesey, and the rest of these gentlemen having asked me to write down the whole particulars about Treasure Island, from the beginning to the end, keeping nothing back but the bearings of the island, and that only because there is still treasure not yet lifted, I take up my pen in the year of grace 17—, and go back to the time when my father kept the "Admiral Benbow" inn, and the brown old seaman, with the sabre cut, first took up his lodging under our roof.⁵⁷

While Stevenson does not provide, through Jim, a lengthy explanation of the book's origins, he does pack quite a bit of information into *Treasure Island*'s first paragraph. Jim declares that he has been assigned this writing task at the request of Trelawney, Livesey, "and the rest of these gentlemen." This opening statement not only positions Jim as a dutiful young person rather than a base, attention-seeker (a conventionally appropriate posture for him to have at the beginning of a travel narrative), but it also indicates that his work has been endorsed by multiple respected gentlemen. A squire, a doctor, "and the rest of the gentlemen" endorse Jim as their preferred communicator and their request adds to his credibility as an eyewitness. In keeping with travel writers' usual pledge of truthfulness, Jim says that the gentlemen asked him "to write down the whole particulars … from the beginning to the end, keeping nothing back but the bearings of the island, and that only because there is still treasure" there. What Jim promises readers, then, is a complete, chronological account with a reasonable exception that Jim makes transparent from the start.

In the space of one sentence, Stevenson manages to present Jim as a credible narrator tasked with honestly reporting events of the past who is also in that very moment taking up his pen to write. Stevenson navigates this retrospective point of view throughout *Treasure Island* as skillfully as Charles Dickens in *David Copperfield* and Charlotte Brontë in *Jane Eyre*, subtly moving between carefully narrated past actions and present-day reflections on that past. A typical example occurs in the first chapter when Jim recounts the arrival of the "old buccaneer," Billy Bones, who arrives at the Hawkins' inn and overstays his welcome. After conveying Bones's threatening manners, "Dreadful stories," and excessive drinking in sharp detail, Jim reflects,

> My father was always saying the inn would be ruined, for people would soon cease coming there to be tyrannised over and put down, and sent shivering to their beds; but I really believe his presence did us good. People were frightened at the time, but on looking back they rather liked it; it was a fine excitement in a quiet country life; and there was even a party of the younger men who pretended to admire him, calling him a "true sea-dog," and a "real old salt," and such like names, and saying there was the sort of man that made England terrible at sea.[58]

These two sentences of reflection typify the style Stevenson crafts for Jim as the book's writer–protagonist. Jim evaluates the event with the benefit of hindsight while also acknowledging how it seemed in the moment, and Stevenson conveys this with subtle complexity. Jim's narration in the above passage is not just a simple past tense, first-person point of view, either: he discusses Bones by quoting other characters in both direct and indirect discourse. Jim notes the men who call Bones a "true sea-dog" and a "real old salt" while also indirectly quoting, "there was the sort of man that made England terrible at sea." And although he does not cite his father directly, one can imagine Jim's father using the language "shivering to their beds" when complaining about Bones's effect on customers at the inn. This kind of narration, which blends past action and speech with present-day reflection and free indirect discourse, collapses the distance between Jim the narrator, writing down this story at the request of his respectable friends, and Jim the witness in the moment, the character navigating the oddities of his family's guest. Readers experience Jim in *and* at a distance from the action. Stevenson manages this kind of temporal slippage and narrative subtlety expertly throughout the novel, taking advantage of Jim's big-picture view as one who has returned from the adventure, while also conveying the exuberance and anxieties of the younger boy not yet aware of where this adventure will take him.

In one of the most dramatic moments in the book, Jim faces a wounded but cunning Israel Hands on board the *Hispaniola*. Jim scrambles up to the cross-trees to get as far away as possible from Hands, who is armed with a dagger. Jim primes his pistols while Hands follows, slowed down by his wounded leg. Now in an advantageous position, Jim confidently aims his ready pistols at his assailant:

> I was drinking in his words and smiling away, as conceited as a cock upon a wall, when, all in a breath, back went his right hand over his shoulder. Something sang like an arrow through the air; I felt a blow and then a sharp pang, and there I was pinned by the shoulder to the mast. In the horrid pain and surprise of the moment—I scarce can say it was by my own volition, and I am sure it was without a conscious aim—both my pistols went off, and both escaped out of my hands. They did not fall alone; with a choked cry, the coxswain loosed his grasp upon the shrouds, and plunged head first into the water.[59]

Stevenson successfully captures the suspense of this standoff and its surprises despite the constraint of working from a retrospective point of view. He nimbly preserves readers' anxiety by holding back certain information that the older Jim writing this text knows. It is not a knife that flies towards him but "Something," the pronoun emphasizing Jim's astonishment at Hand's quick action and keeping readers in the extraordinary moment along with the young Jim. Readers are brought out of the action only briefly with the writer–protagonist's interjection to defend his shooting of Hands: "I scarce can say it was by my own volition, and I am sure it was without a conscious aim." In some ways, this interruption is risky. What passes between Jim Hawkins and Israel Hands elevated above the deck can only last a matter of seconds, which Stevenson conveys with paced words like "all in a breath," "blow," "pang," "surprise of the moment" and "plunged." For Stevenson to suspend the velocity of this exchange could weaken the moment's power. But Jim's interjection adroitly informs readers in the midst of the action that this shooting has weighed upon his mind. He has had to think back on the death of Hands and wonder if he intended to kill the man or if he pulled the triggers instinctually in his surprise. Like the previously discussed passage about Billy Bones, Stevenson places Jim and readers in the action while also delicately reminding us of Jim's position outside of it. Bird defended her decision to retain the letter format of her travel books because she believed they offered readers an opportunity to feel a part of the journey at the time. She wanted to provide them, or at least make them feel as though she provided them, an initial impression of things. Stevenson achieves this in *Treasure Island* through rich yet constrained prose. The vividness of Jim "as conceited as a cock upon a wall" blends together with the frightening generality of "Something [singing] like an arrow through the air." The retrospective memoir form of this book affords Stevenson the opportunity to play with that tension between the uncertainty of a present moment and the perceptiveness of hindsight. Once again, Stevenson manages to achieve what seems difficult to do in a constraining form. He creates a sense of intimacy with the writer–protagonist without sacrificing a sense of breadth. Readers understandably feel connected to Jim since he is the book's narrator, and even though this narrative point of view significantly limits what readers can see, Jim's narration does not feel curtailed.

At least until it is curtailed. If we get lulled into the comforts of Stevenson's agile prose, we are jolted out of it later in the novel when the narrative makes a significant shift. At the end of Part III, Jim encounters "The Man of the Island," Ben Gunn, for the first time. Out on his own, desperate, and convinced that he has "nothing left" except "death by starvation, or death by the hands of the mutineers,"[60] Jim hears "a spout of gravel … dislodged" and turns to see who or what caused the sound. He sees "a figure leap" but cannot determine whether this "creature" is an "apparition," "bear or man or monkey."[61] This is, of course, a moment of high tension in the novel as Jim is already endangered and is now encountering another possible foe. Having been marooned on the island three years ago, Gunn has survived on goats, berries, and oysters and claims to be rich. Despite Gunn's pledge to "make a man of you, Jim"[62] and to help in his "clove hitch,"[63] we are not totally sure what Gunn intends because Jim, our trusted narrator, does not know what to make of him. After Gunn describes how he got on the island and has given Jim some instructions to follow, Jim replies, "Well … I don't understand one word that you've been saying."[64] This reply operates as a release valve for readers (i.e., we have not understood Gunn, but neither has the novel's writer–protagonist, so we are in good company), and it heightens suspense at a key moment. Just as readers and Jim are puzzled by Gunn's passionate directives, a cannon goes off, indicating that the fighting has begun between Jim's friends and the mutineers. Gunn and Jim take off running towards the action.

Here Stevenson drastically alters the novel's point of view, switching narrators for the next three chapters. Alexandra Valint calls this moment a "quick switch" as Dr. Livesey becomes the narrator, and it dramatically reminds readers of the limitations of a first-person point of view.[65] At a moment when Jim is running towards danger alongside a man whose sanity remains in question, we are forced to leave him. The three chapters labeled "Narrative Continued by the Doctor" cover "How the Ship Was Abandoned," "The Jolly-Boat's Last Trip," and "End of the First Day's Fighting." These are certainly important moments in the book's documentation of the struggle between Captain Smollett's loyal men and Long John Silver's mutineers, but because Stevenson has trained our sympathies on Jim up to this point the shift to Livesey is rather jarring. While Stevenson's narrative switch may simply allow him to fill in some of the plot while Jim is away from his friends, it also reminds us how limited our perspective has been. Jim's narration has been so rich with detail that readers may have forgotten the documentary premise of the novel and its inherent constraints. Livesey's narration reminds readers of those constraints, that, as compelling and intimate as Jim's point of view is, it remains only his point of view, and it has significant, unavoidable blind spots. Stevenson's employment of a second narrator is a continuation of his crafting of *Treasure Island* as a fake travel narrative. Like the color map that supposedly authenticates the journey and preserves the notes of people in the book, this shift to Livesey nudges readers, reminding them that Jim cannot be in all places at all times. It is a kind of brief admission of the form's constraints, an internal certification of the narrative's legitimacy.

Stevenson's achievements in *Treasure Island* reveal an intentional engagement with the conventions of Victorian travel writing even as the novelist surpasses what we may have thought possible in the subgenre. Rather than feeling overdone, predictable, and lazy, *Treasure Island* bristles with energy and innovation. Stevenson deploys the conventions of the fake travel narrative with great intention, exploits their latent potentialities, integrates them with surprisingly nuanced prose, and expertly manages to balance the familiar and the strange in every aspect of the novel.

If Stevenson's adventure novels show us the elasticity of documentary travel writing, then H. Rider Haggard's show us how the elastic can snap tightly back into place. Haggard's novels generally lack the nuanced and balanced innovation of Stevenson's, even though Haggard explicitly attempted to write like him. Stevenson admittedly stole from Poe, Marryat, and Irving, and Haggard follows right him behind in line. The story goes that

> one of Rider's brothers asked his opinion of an adventure story that had just been published, *Treasure Island*, and Rider replied recklessly that, although it was certainly a good tale, he himself could write a boy's book just as good. His brother challenged him, and for the next six weeks Rider spent his evenings ... trying to win the wager with a tale of African adventure. Cassells, who had published *Treasure Island*, agreed to publish *King Solomon's Mines* (1885).[66]

Superficially speaking, the similarities are there: the reluctant and inexperienced eyewitness narrator, the hunt for riches, the difficult to interpret map, and the all-male team that sets out for unknown territory.

Despite these similarities, however, Stevenson's and Haggard's documentary novels differ dramatically in terms of their authenticity claims and narrative style. On this subject, C. S. Lewis offers a useful characterization of Haggard's writing that helps distinguish it from Stevenson's. He writes,

The lack of detailed character-study is not a fault at all. An adventure story neither needs nor admits it. Even in real life adventures tend to obliterate fine shades. Hardship and danger strip us down to the bare moral essentials. The distinction between shirker and helper, brave and cowardly, trusty and treacherous, overrides everything else. "Character" in the novelist's sense is a flower that expands fully where people are safe, fed, dry, and warmed. That adventure stories remind us of this is one of their merits. The real defects of Haggard are two. First, he can't write. Or rather (I learn from Mr Cohen) won't. Won't be bothered. Hence the *clichés*, jocosities, frothy eloquence.[67]

More recently, Nathan Hensley, in his 2016 book *Forms of Empire: The Poetics of Victorian Sovereignty*, termed Haggard "Victorian literature's clumsiest stylist."[68] While some readers may disagree with Lewis's and Hensley's assessments, they strikingly embody the inverse of what Sleigh praises in Stevenson's prose. Stevenson's writing is limpid, accurate, and tightly tracked while Haggard's is frothy and clichéd even when given the allowance of foregoing characterization. Stevenson employs some paratextual elements common to travel writing in creating an atmosphere of authenticity in *Treasure Island* and *Kidnapped*, but his prose tends to do more of the heavy lifting in terms of establishing a sense of verisimilitude. As I have argued, he expertly manages the limitations of a first-person, retrospective narrator, and crafts novels that recognizably fit within the established norms of Victorian travel writing but also expand our understanding of its affordances.

Ultimately, Haggard fails to capitalize on the potentialities of first-person narration as effectively as Stevenson and instead relies more heavily on the paratextual conventions of Victorian travel and adventure writing to give his work an air of authenticity. Haggard leans heavily into the documentary proofs of the subgenre, playing with non-fiction editorial practices to frame his far-flung and far-fetched adventures. Even with the froth and clichés Lewis identifies and bemoans, Haggard's novels still demonstrate a range of entertaining and engaging possibilities that the documentary form affords.

Perhaps the best example of Haggard's playful engagement with paratextual elements is in *She: A History of Adventure* in which it is as if he

Figure 3.2: "Facsimile of the Sherd of Amenartas"; "Facsimile of the Reverse of the Sherd of Amenartas," plates preceding title page. H. Rider Haggard, *She: A History of Adventure*. London: Longmans, Green and Co., 1887. *Visual Haggard*

has pulled out all the stops in terms of drawing attention to the book's plausibility. As Andrew M. Stauffer writes in his introduction to the Broadview edition, the novel is "the work of an author concerned with authenticity and the craft of storytelling."[69] Haggard displays this concern by establishing an apparatus for the novel that supposedly includes his editorial fingerprint as well as that of a central character, Horace Holly. Like Stevenson's novels, *She* was serialized before being sold in a single volume, appearing in weekly installments in *The Graphic* from October 1886 through January 1887. The first UK edition, published in 1887, "included a 2-page frontispiece of the Sherd of Amenartas, which Haggard drew with the help of his sister-in-law, Miss Barber."[70] Like the map Stevenson created for *Treasure Island*, the frontispiece of *She* is worth seeing in full color, as before the narrative even begins, this "History of

Adventure" presents itself as a trove of authentic, historical, and archaeo-logical artifacts.[71] The facsimiles of the sherd are complete with labeling on the length, breadth, and weight of the original and scale of the repro-duced image ("ONE ½ SIZE"), similar to what one would see in a museum catalog or textbook (see Figure 3.2). Like the map of Treasure Island, the sherd is not a mere ornamentation to the novel, but is a source of action in the book and a visual representation of an adventure's history, with the sherd's "numerous inscriptions … of the most erratic character" that "had clearly been made by different hands and in many different ages."[72]

Haggard does not limit his use of these kinds of documentary proofs to his novel's endpapers, however, as he also embeds them into the narra-tive through his role as supposed editor. In the novel's "Introduction," Haggard begins, "I may as well say at once that I am not the narrator but only the editor of this extraordinary history," and goes on to describe how this story came to him.[73] Five years after meeting an exceedingly hand-some and an exceedingly ugly man on the street and discussing "the Zulu people," Haggard receives "a letter and two packets, one of manuscript."[74] This letter, included for readers to see, explains that these two men, Horace Holly and his ward Leo Vincey, experienced "a real African adventure" that the enclosed manuscript describes. In keeping with the tradition of travel writing of pledging reluctance and honesty, Holly divulges to Haggard that the two had intended to keep the story private, but, ultimately unsure on what to do, the men request that Haggard read the manuscript and decide whether the public deserves to know the story, promising "that everything is described … exactly as it happened."[75]

All of this should sound familiar: the posture of authenticity, the reluctant writer, the distrust of a public audience, and the claim of abso-lute honesty. Like Bird, Seacole, Stanley, and Kingsley, Haggard hits these conventional notes, establishing the book's premise with readers and setting their expectations for what follows. Echoing Defoe's editorial state-ment in *Robinson Crusoe*, Haggard writes, "To me the story seems to bear the stamp of truth upon its face," and, echoing the supposed editors of Wilkie Collins's casebook novels, adds, "Of the history itself the reader must judge."[76]

In addition to these preliminary comments about the manuscript's authenticity, Haggard inserts documentary evidence into the narrative through footnotes and transcriptions or visual reproductions of artifacts, typically conventions of non-fiction writing. Some of the footnotes that interrupt the narrative are signed by Holly while others are signed by the "EDITOR"—Haggard. The footnotes not only mark the book as a serious work of non-fiction, but they also serve as a reference check on the material that Haggard uses to enhance the novel's claim of authenticity. For instance, early in the novel when Holly and Leo are examining the sherd, Holly speculates

> Whether this was the cartouche of the original Kallikrates,[1] or of some Prince or Pharaoh from whom his wife Amenartas was descended, I am not sure.

The corresponding footnote to Holly's conjecture reads:

> [1] The cartouche, if it be a true cartouche, cannot have been that of Kallikrates, as Mr. Holly suggests. Kallikrates was a priest and not entitled to a cartouche, which was the prerogative of Egyptian royalty, though he might have inscribed his name or title upon an *oval.*—EDITOR.[77]

This fact check of the manuscript continues the façade of the history book in conjunction with the detailed descriptions of these artifacts and the facsimiles that capture the physical appearance of the lettering on the sherd and the composition scarab. Oscar Wilde comments on Haggard's use of footnotes in "The Decay of Lying" (1891), as Vivian bemoans the lack of lying in art, stating, "As for Mr Rider Haggard, who really has, or had once, the makings of a perfectly magnificent liar, he is now so afraid of being suspected of genius that when he does tell us anything marvellous, he feels bound to invent a personal reminiscence, and to put it into a foot-note as a kind of cowardly corroboration."[78] For Wilde, Haggard's posture as an editor of historical and verifiable materials is an insult to art, which should be "indifferent to fact" and "invents, imagines, dreams, and keeps between herself and reality the impenetrable barrier of beautiful style, or decorative or ideal treatment."[79] Never mind the fact that Haggard's editorial posturing is a sham and part of the fictional world he has created,

Wilde prefers fiction to be unconcerned with verifying its relationship to truth—even when does so disingenuously.[80]

The footnotes by Holly also allow him to reflect on or contextualize beyond what he provides in the main narrative. The most extraordinary example of this type appears much later in the novel when Holly is trying to decide if he thinks Ayesha is evil. He offers one position in the main body of text but then offers another in a long footnote that takes up nearly half the page. This split between the main narrative and the discursive footnote neatly illustrates how Haggard's writing differs from Stevenson's. As I previously discussed, Stevenson is able to capture Jim Hawkins's past and current selves in *Treasure Island* with impressive subtlety within Jim's narration of the adventure. Haggard, less skilled in this kind of nuanced point of view, must split up Holly's past self and his more current understanding between the main text and the footnote that interrupts it. Both writers seek to expose a sense of the narrator's ambivalence, but Haggard achieves this through blunter mechanical means than Stevenson by utilizing the device of a footnote.

Haggard's tendency to employ these kinds of supplemental instruments opened him up to be cheaply mimicked and parodied.[81] One parody of *King Solomon's Mines*, for example, published in 1887, titled *King Solomon's Wives; Or, the Phantom Mines* by "Hyder Ragged," mocks Haggard's almost obsessive claims of authenticity. The book contains a color map with seemingly genuine symbols and opens with a description of its purpose (see Figure 3.3a and b):

> Now that this book is printed, and about to be given to the world, the question will perhaps arise—Why do I write it? Captious people may suggest—For reasons not unconnected with the paltry pence which its sale may produce. Such suggestions I repel with scorn. My reason—I give it without hesitation—is this: To prove my veracity."[82]

This posture pinpoints Haggard's overemphasis on authenticity by joking that it is the central purpose of the book (rather than, say, to share a fun adventure), and, in keeping with other works of Victorian travel writing, the author excessively claims to have pure motives. In the illustration

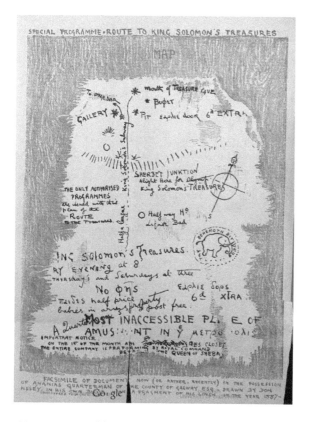

Figure 3.3a and b: Hyder Ragged, *King Solomon's Wives; Or, the Phantom Mines*. London: Vizetelly & Co., 1887. University of California Libraries

INTRODUCTION.

OW that this book is printed, and about to be given to the world, the question will perhaps arise— Why do I write it? Captious people may suggest—For reasons not unconnected with the paltry pence which its sale may produce. Such suggestions I repel with scorn. My reason—I give it without hesitation—is this: To prove my veracity. The one quality for which my family has always been noted is its unswerving veracity. A Quarterman's word has always been as good as his bond. I have never heard our greatest enemy

KING SOLOMON'S WIVES;

OR,

THE PHANTOM MINES.

~~~~~~•♦•~~~~~~

CHAPTER I.

MY PLAN OF THE CAMPAIGN—I MEET SIR HARRY—
THE VOYAGE OUT.

 ALES of mysterious adventure have always been my delight. Having come to the conclusion,* from a careful perusal of some of the more recent of these histories, that the

* *Note by* EDITOR : Why, you have only just begun !
Note by ME : Am I writing this book, or you ?
Note by EDITOR : Very sorry ; only my fun.
Note by ME : It may be your idea of fun ; it is not mine.
Don't let it occur again.

Figure 3.4: Opening page. Hyder Ragged, *King Solomon's Wives;
Or, the Phantom Mines.* London: Vizetelly & Co., 1887.
University of California Libraries

accompanying the "Introduction," Quarterman (a thinly veiled play on Quatermain) holds an arm out against payment for his writing, suggesting that the writer has not been motivated by profit to write down this account. Throughout the book's chapters, "Ragged" uses footnotes, ridiculing Haggard's use of this non-fiction tool and the novelist's artificially crafted status of editor. At the beginning of chapter 1, the "EDITOR" argues on the page with "ME" (see Figure 3.4), making Haggard's professed editorial role look like an absurd, cheap trick.

This parody underscores not only how Haggard's tactics could be easily deployed elsewhere but also the durability and transferability of the conventions of adventure and travel writing more broadly. The impetus to establish credibility, pledge honesty, admit limitations, and present proof cuts across non-fiction and fiction in these nineteenth-century books and ranges from books that contain nuanced writing to parodies with cheap punchlines. Stevenson pairs a selection of predictable conventions with captivating, innovative prose while Haggard playfully exploits the affordances of footnotes, mapping, framing, and archeological evidence almost to excess. When considered this way, the norms of these travel and adventure novels seem more flexible than they might initially appear considering the durability of these conventions. These novels seem bound to documents and displayed proofs of the journeys taken, but they are not beholden to one manner of exploiting them.

The Chain of Mimicry

In this chapter I have emphasized the tight chain of mimicry from non-fiction travel writers to novelists and their parodists and argued that these authors all utilized firmly established conventions of travel and adventure writing, evincing a robust and fixed trait pattern. They crafted postures of reluctant authenticity and employed paratextual elements to enhance a sense of the real, working to imaginatively transport readers into far-flung locales. It should be noted that we can trace this chain of mimicry back long before the nineteenth century—back even to the earliest novels in the English language by Daniel Defoe and Aphra Behn.

When we trace this lineage, of course, we also follow a history of British imperialism. Since Edward Said's groundbreaking work, scholars have recognized and grappled with the novel's role in promoting imperialist ideology and normalizing British hegemony. In *Culture and Imperialism* (1993) Said claims, "Nearly everywhere in nineteenth- and early-twentieth-century British and French culture we find allusions to the facts of empire, but perhaps nowhere with more regularity and frequency than in the British novel. Taken together, these allusions constitute what I have called a structure of attitude and reference."[83] Victorian travel and adventure novels, taking place in outposts of empire or the supposedly blank places of the earth assuredly participate in building that structure of attitude and reference. These novels concern themselves with "sustained possession, with far-flung and sometimes unknown spaces, with eccentric or unacceptable human begins, with fortune-enhancing or fantasized activities like emigration, money-making, and sexual adventure."[84] Haggard's imperial romances, in particular, repeatedly feature white male heroes who triumph over exotic and frequently sexualized landscapes and people.

But what if we associate imperialism with Victorian travel and adventure documentary novels not only because of their subject matter and setting but also because of their form? What if these documentary novels are a fitting vehicle for racist ideology, at least in part, because of their chain of mimicry—the way they seem to copy each other? The firmly established trait pattern of documentary evidence like maps and illustrations, the posturing of a trustworthy and usually white reporter (Mary Seacole being an important exception), and the stark contrast between the known metropole and the mysterious and dangerous wilderness helps crystalize harmful ideas about colonial lands and subjects. Tropes and stereotypes form through repetition, and the chain of mimicry across Victorian travel and adventure writing, or what Said calls "regularity and frequency," only enhances the sense of an entrenched and seemingly natural power dynamic.

Homi Bhabha's work on mimicry adds another layer of complexity here. For while he draws our attention to the way mimicry is "a complex strategy of reform, regulation and discipline, which 'appropriates' the Other as it visualizes power," Bhabha also emphasizes "that mimicry is at once resemblance and menace."[85] "The *menace* of mimicry," he writes, "is its *double* vision which in disclosing the ambivalence of colonial discourse also disrupts its authority."[86] Bhabha considers the repetition of stereotypes as both "anxious" and "assertive, declaring what is 'known' about the native but nonetheless anxiously restating this knowledge as if it can never be confirmed but only reinforced through constant repetition, making it a sign of a deeper crisis of authority in the wielding of colonial power."[87]

What does this mean, then, when we note that British travel and adventure novels not only repeat plots and character types but also their documentary form with its premise of an on-the-ground informant? The vessel of these repetitions is the copied and re-copied form of the travel journal, memoir, or found document. Could it be that Victorian travel and adventure novels embody "resemblance and menace" not only in the repetition of story elements, exotic settings, and character types but also in the repeated use of the documentary form to convey such stories? I believe so.

The form of these novels inherently privileges the perspective of the white and male writer–protagonist, whose vision of the world and his role in it dominates the narrative. The form's inclusion of documentary evidence as part of its historical posturing further entrenches the notion of an established hierarchy and pattern of engagement with the world. The regularity and frequency of the form's established conventions—the amateur or reluctant writer–traveler, the use of non-fiction elements like editorial notes, illustrations, and maps, and preserved or found documentary evidence—reinforce through repetition the empire's capacity to gaze, record, and contain. If Bhabha is right, though, that repetition illustrates crisis as well as confidence, we might consider these novels as evidence not only of Britain's imperial power but also its anxieties about that power.

My suggestion that we consider the form of these novels as well as their content when we think about the history and legacy of British imperialism is important as we push to "undiscipline" the field of Victorian studies. As Ronjaunee Chatterjee, Alicia Mireles Christoff, and Amy R. Wong write in their introduction to a special issue of *Victorian Studies* on the subject, there are "troubling de facto social segregations" in the field: "brown bodies are ghettoized in so-called special interest panels on postcolonial topics and spaces, while general interest panels focus on seemingly more neutral subjects such as form and reading—often code, we suggest, for a latent and unexamined whiteness."[88] The question I raise here about travel and adventure fiction's repeated use of the documentary form destabilizes the presumption that form is automatically race-neutral or that form exists beyond the reach of harmful human ideologies. These novels require a communicating eyewitness and thus more often than not privilege "Eurocentricity and its attendant whiteness."[89] The very structure of these texts embeds a perspectival bias, and our attention to the documentary form of travel and adventure writing accordingly cannot ignore its potential for harm even as we praise its aesthetic accomplishments and potentialities.

CHAPTER FOUR

Casebook Novels

A Crucial Asset

Perhaps no subgenre exploits so effectively the affordances of documentary fiction than what I call casebook novels of the Victorian period. While each chapter of this book emphasizes the assets of documentary epistolary, life-writing, and adventure novels and describes how authors creatively navigate each mode's limitations, one could argue that these achievements pale in comparison to those made in casebook writing. Or rather, to be more accurate, one could say that the limitations of documentary writing are perfectly suited to casebook novels because these books rely heavily upon narrative concealment and explore the limitations of human knowledge and experience. The limited point-of-view of this type of documentary novel helps make the book a mystery or thriller; it builds suspense, obscures a secret, and provides a valance of objectivity in the wake of a crime, malicious threat, or scandal. In short, the tightly restricted point-of-view and document-bound narration is a crucial asset rather than a limitation, and the novels I discuss in this chapter benefit significantly from the documentary form in which they are written: Wilkie Collins's *The Woman in White* (1859–60) and *The Moonstone* (1868), Charles Warren Adams's *The Notting Hill Mystery* (1862–63), and Bram Stoker's *Dracula* (1897). Furthermore, the form of these novels document epistemological uncertainty, their fake materials emphasizing the linguistic and material challenges in capturing the horrific. They simultaneously represent a desire to "pin down" the truth through the inclusion of compelling evidence yet they also plainly exhibit the difficulty or even impossibility of doing so.

I am not the first to discuss these novels together or note their similarities and strengths as documentary fiction. Roger Luckhurst in his introduction to the Oxford World's Classics edition of *Dracula* writes that *The Woman in White* "was Stoker's obvious model" for the novel, and he situates the vampire novel within the Gothic tradition in which "excesses are often given fictitious framings as manuscripts or a mass of fragmentary evidence carefully collated by increasingly terrified editors."[1] A. B. Emrys links *The Woman in White*, *The Moonstone*, and *Dracula* together as testimonial novels,[2] and Katrien Bollen and Raphaël Ingelbien suggest reading Stoker's vampire novel "as a response to *The Woman in White*" claiming that "[t]o late-Victorian reviewers, the 'fragmentary' form of *Dracula* was neither experimental nor proto-modernist (as these labels would obviously have been anachronistic), but simply harked back to a well-tried formula of Victorian sensational fiction."[3] Lara Karpenko writes that *The Notting Hill Mystery* "clearly seems inspired by *The Woman in White* and other early sensation novels" as well, and Adams's novel is regularly discussed in conjunction with *The Moonstone* as early examples of English detective novels.

This chapter highlights these novels' achievements despite the limitations of the documentary form to further underscore the thesis of this book—that Victorian novelists utilized a range of affordances of documentary writing—and my rationale for calling them casebook novels although they have been referred to by a number of names in literary criticism over the decades. As I discuss later in this chapter, literary critics have embraced these casebook novels and their form with much more enthusiasm than many other subgenres of Victorian documentary novels, so I also detail why these books have been seen as successful, while others—particularly epistolary novels—have been seen as strained and out of fashion. I conclude that these novels wrestle with the status of documentable evidence and their capacity to convey the truth of the cases they narrate. I build, then, on what Elisha Cohn has argued about Collins's *The Moonstone*: "Collins imagines reading not as a paradigm for the pursuit of knowledge, but as a practice that indicates the limitations of knowledge itself."⁴ As such, these novels, although thoroughly recognizable as Victorian, are as much aligned with postmodern ideas about fragmentation, subjectivity, and absolute Truth. In the pages that follow, I highlight the casebook's affordances and the various ways these authors utilize them to build suspense, shield our vision, create intimacy, and explore the limitations of documentary proof. To effectively underscore their shared characteristics, I have organized the chapter by these qualities instead of by author or novel. Consequently, I move from text to text to demonstrate their commonalities rather than discussing one novel at a time.

Defining and Naming the Subgenre

Casebook novels, as I define them, are narrated entirely through a collection of documents and witness testimonies that sum up a case or serve as a kind of brief arguing for the innocence or guilt of a particular party. I use the term "*casebook*" in keeping with the *Oxford English Dictionary*, which defines it as a "book containing records of legal, medical, or other cases," and the form has a rich history in England.⁵ According to the creators of the Casebooks Project at Cambridge University, "The term 'casebook' was initially used for legal records in the late seventeenth century, then applied to doctors' notes in the mid-eighteenth century." The records digitized by the Cambridge group are medical and astrological in nature, as doctors in the 1500s "modelled themselves on Hippocrates, the ancient father of medicine, who had reputedly recorded case histories on clay tablets." As the editors describe,

> Surviving casebooks take a variety of forms. Some are like account books, written at the time of the encounter. Others, like journals or diaries, were written when a doctor returned to his study after a day of visiting patients. Some doctors digested their account books or diaries into observations, narrating the history of the disease and cure, then discarded the rougher, more immediate notes. Whatever form casebooks took, they typically included a date, the patient's name, age, complaint, its causes, a prescription, or a payment.⁶

What they describe is a flexible form of writing that could take on characteristics of other forms like account books and diaries. Although they served a clear purpose in medical practice, they could be a composite collection, documenting different kinds of information. Casebook novels of the Victorian period are thus a recognizable descendent of this form and its possibilities and limitations. Inherent in the casebook is a quality of miscellany. A doctor's casebook, for instance, may include diagnostic information, personal reflection, prescription information, and account records.

The documents included in casebook *novels* supposedly communicate the truth of the case because they feature the voices and perspectives of people directly involved. The novelists invite readers to imagine that these documents, collected by an editor, could come to stand as a type of proof in some sort of legal proceeding or attempt to address a crime extralegally. Here I outline the terms that have been used to describe these novels but argue against their adequacy in emphasizing the books' document-based narration and multi-authored engagement with the precarity of their materials. In doing so I will also highlight some of the unique qualities of this form that makes it so suitable for mystery, sensation, and horror fiction.

One might be tempted to call these books "*testimonial*" or "*eyewitness*" novels because they feature written statements from characters, but that name suggests a uniformity of documents.[7] One of the distinguishing characteristics of casebook novels, as I am defining them, is that they are collections of various types of documents. Their contents do not include a single form like a witness testimony. Rather, they consist of statements, memoranda, newspaper clippings, telegrams, letters, diary entries, doctors' notes, and, in at least one instance, the testimony of a tombstone.[8] These novels are not merely multi-voice, they are multi-text.[9]

"*Testimonial*" can also suggest that the document's writer intends for the material to be used as testimony. While that is the case for some, like the narratives in *The Moonstone*, it is not the case for all of them. Marian Halcombe's diary, whose pages constitute a large portion of *The Woman in White*, was not composed with the intention of serving in any kind of legal or authoritative capacity. Her diary was composed for her own personal use. Similarly, in *Dracula*, John Seward's notes "Kept in phonograph" on his patient Renfield are composed for his own diagnostic study and betterment as a physician—not because he was asked to provide them.[10] Likewise, Ralph Henderson, the life insurance investigator who compiles the documents making up *The Notting Hill Mystery*, includes private correspondence and journal entries composed without knowledge that there would ever be such a grave inquiry. This, of course, does not preclude the documents from being used as evidence. Alexander Welsh writes in *Strong Representations: Narrative and Circumstantial Evidence in England* (1992), "All evidence, in short, has to be read or interpreted as such. Yet it need not be instigated by anyone or originate from a conscious act." In fact, this can be seen as an asset: "One of the main advantages of circumstantial evidence, often remarked, is precisely this freedom from human deliberation at the origin."[11] In other words, part of what makes these documents so compelling as evidence is their circumstantiality; they were not composed with a detective mission in mind. Many of the materials these novels include are documents that were originally intended as private, and they imbue each work with a sense of intimacy and shortsightedness. Seward cannot know when he is recording his notes that Renfield's condition connects to the vampire; Mrs. Anderton cannot perceive when writing in her journal that her illness is the result of a premeditated crime. The limited view of these documents contributes to the novels' suspense and the productive tension between what the characters do not know and what the reader begins to suspect. More than mere flash of dramatic irony, these documents create a sense of unease that permeates the novels.

Calling these novels casebooks emphasizes the diversity of their content, and this is a key feature because every type of document included in these novels has a purpose and style that aligns with the conventions of each particular form. Marian's diary, for example, though it becomes valuable evidence in *The Woman in White*'s documentation of Sir Percival Glyde's crimes and Laura Fairlie's true identity, was not designed as witness testimony, so it bears the hallmarks of the form in which she wrote it. Diary entries are reflective, calendar and event driven, and private; letters are private documents composed for an intended recipient; telegrams deliver short, urgent messages; tombstones offer summation and finality. Analyzing the narrative style of these novels, then, requires considering the possibilities, limitations, and conventions of each document's form when evaluating the novelist's choice in creating a multi-voice and multi-text casebook and the ways these forms work together as a collection, forming consensuses as well as troubling discrepancies and gaps.

One powerful example of this occurs in Marian's diary extracts about halfway through *The Woman in White*. Marian narrates the novel through private, almost daily, entries for nearly 200 pages in a modern edition (twelve weeks of issues in the original *All the Year Round* serialization).[12] A diary's regular, linear renderings of a day's events engenders a sense of intimacy and trust with readers, and the eager *All the Year Round* readers received access to thoughts Marian shares with no one. She is the "eyes" of the novel for months and our key window into life at Blackwater Park.[13] In her final entry, she is feverish and panicked after eavesdropping on Glyde and Count Fosco, and recognizing their devilish, mercenary intentions towards Lady Glyde and Anne Catherick. Because of Marian's careful documentation of Laura's painful married life, and their disturbing experiences with the Count, readers' fears for these women are now at their highest pitch. Collins takes advantage of the regularity of diary writing to build up our trust in Marian and our desire to protect her—to keep another entry coming with each passing, disturbing day—but her writing becomes increasingly clipped and distressed, and the document ends in an alarming manner:

> My head—I am sadly afraid of my head. I can write, but the lines all run together. I see the words. Laura—I can write Laura, and see I write it. Eight or nine—which was it?
>
> So cold, so cold—oh, that rain last night!—and the strokes of the clock, the strokes I can't count, keep striking in my head——
>
> * * *
>
> NOTE.
>
> [At this place the entry in the Diary ceases to be legible. The two or three lines which follow, contain fragments of words only, mingled with blots and scratches of the pen. The last marks on the paper bear some resemblance to the first two letters (L and A) of the name of Lady Glyde.
>
> On the next page of the Diary, another entry appears. It is in a man's handwriting, large, bold, and firmly regular; and the date is "June the 21st." It contains these lines:]

POSTSCRIPT BY A SINCERE FRIEND

The illness of our excellent Miss Halcombe has afforded me the opportunity of enjoying an unexpected intellectual pleasure.

I refer to the perusal (which I have just completed) of this interesting Diary.

There are many hundred pages here. I can lay my hand on my heart, and declare that every page has charmed, refreshed, delighted me.

To a man of my sentiments, it is unspeakably gratifying to be able to say this.

Admirable woman!

I allude to Miss Halcombe.

Stupendous effort!

I refer to the Diary.

Yes! these pages are amazing.[14]

The writer of these lines, of course, is the man Marian has overheard colluding with Percival Glyde. Fosco's overtaking of Marian's diary at such a moment of vulnerability is shocking in its force and one that Collins crafted to be read as an awful violation. Fosco not only discloses that he has read the diary with Marian's private opinions, musings, and fears, but he also takes up the pen himself to write in "handwriting, large, bold, and firmly regular," much in contrast to Marian's illegible "fragments" and "blots and scratches of the pen."[15] Readers know that Marian has long feared the Count's manipulations, power, and knowledge, so his reading of her diary is particularly wounding.

The postscript highlights elements of Fosco's character we already recognize, like his vanity, but, more importantly, it reveals at a key moment how Collins masterfully takes advantage of the collective force of this multi-voice, multi-text casebook form. The multi-voice documents form a collection, but they do not necessarily form consensus. Fosco's writing in Marian's diary is a jarring unplugging, a terrifying turn of the lock in a dark room. The reader's terror at Fosco's silencing of Marian comes as the result of Collins's self-conscious use of a diary as his narrative vehicle. Not designed as testimony but as private record of thoughts and experiences, Marian's diary entries have connected readers intimately to her and aligned our perspectives with her. Fosco's reading and defiling of her diary works narratively because Collins has expertly managed the limitations and possibilities of this personal document's form.

Similarly, in *Dracula*, Stoker uses an array of documents that were not intended to be public, and he advantageously employs a variety of writing conventions when plotting the novel and creating moments of heightened tension. Although the documents of *The Woman in White*, *The Moonstone*, and *The Notting Hill Mystery* are collected in the aftermath of the case, *Dracula* traces the compilation of the novel's documents in the heat of the action, with Mina and Jonathan typing everything "in chronological order" to build "a whole connected narrative," as Dr. Seward describes it in his diary.[16] Much of what gets included in Mina's and Jonathan's transcriptions of events was not intended for public reading. In fact, all of the documents of *Dracula* (and there are many), except the newspaper clippings from "'The Dailygraph', 8 AUGUST,"[17] "'The Pall Mall Gazette', 18 September,"[18] "The 'Westminster Gazette', 25 September,"[19] and "The 'Westminster Gazette', 25 September, Extra Special,"[20] were written to be either private (in a diary or journal) or read by an identified correspondent (in a letter, telegram, or memorandum). Thus, these documents provide not only first-person narration, but also, as in Collins's and Adams's novels, the characteristics particular to each form in terms of content, style, length, and purpose. The personal documents of *Dracula*, which make up the vast majority of the novel, are written with the assumption of privacy or of reaching their intended recipient. This is plain enough, but Stoker constructs and arranges these documents strategically so that their order not only provides a timeline of the action (as Mina says, "In this matter dates are everything")[21] but also indicates poignant moments of failure, suspense, and human or technological limitation.

One technique Stoker uses to great effect in this arena is that of a personal document that was intended for a correspondent but that was never delivered or opened by such person. Mina, for example, writes a letter to Lucy Westenra dated September 17, in which she informs her friend of Jonathan's recent promotion to partner and inquires about the health of her mother and the status of her wedding planning. As a letter, it is specific in its commentary and questions, directed specifically to the recipient who is a long-term correspondent, so the letter fittingly builds upon previous exchanges of information between the two young women. It contains mostly personal information and conveys joy and curiosity—a tone in keeping with the relationship built between the two. In short, it reads like a real letter, and on its surface has nothing much to distinguish it. The timing and fate of this letter, however, is everything, and Stoker's construction and placement of it after the "Memorandum Left by Lucy Westenra" in which she tells of the horrifying night when her mother dies and she is attacked, and then Dr. Seward's descriptions of their failure to bring Lucy back to health, means that Mina's letter arrives at a moment of heightened tension: readers know Lucy is near death while Mina does not. Stoker's labeling of two documents, divided by a report to Dr. Seward on Renfield, as "*Letter, Mina Harker to Lucy Westenra* (Unopened by her)," posted just a day apart, builds up the reader's concern that Lucy has indeed died. Crucially, the suspense built in this moment does not derive from the contents of the letters but from their limited perspective (Mina's unawareness of Lucy's declining health) and their failure in reaching the intended recipient. In "The Narrative Method of *Dracula*," David Seed writes that Stoker creates "a narrative in which the gaps between the narrating documents become as important as the sections of narrative proper."[22] I will amend Seed's comment slightly and add that the types of documents Stoker uses and their conventions often determine the power of those narrative gaps as much as the contents of the documents themselves. In other words, their form inevitably impacts their function. Or, as Caroline Levine writes, "materiality is determinant."[23]

The term "*casebook*" aptly conveys the impact that the pastiche documentary form of Collins's, Adams's, and Stoker's novels have on readers. As I earlier claimed, the terms "*testimonial*" and "*eyewitness*" suggest a uniformity of documents and the characters' intention for their material to be used as testimony. *Dracula*'s multi-voice, multi-text form—its "mass of type-writing," as Jonathan calls it[24]—hardly fits any definition of uniformity, and, as Seed stresses, it is often the gaps and silences—the moments when there is not an eyewitness in *Dracula*—that are so powerful. Mina does not know what has happened to Lucy, and Stoker uses that lack of knowledge to build suspense and heighten the emotional impact of the vampire's atrocious actions.

Of the novels discussed here, *The Moonstone* best fits the category of "*eyewitness*" novel because most of its narratives were written and collected to be witness statements. Additionally, Collins's characters use the term "*witness*" to describe themselves, and they clearly and repeatedly state their understanding that their writing has a particular scope and purpose. As Gabriel Betteredge writes, "In this matter of the Moonstone the plan is, not to present reports, but to produce witnesses."[25] Later, Miss Clack, in a wonderfully entertaining section of the novel, expresses frustration at the restricted scope and purpose of the material she has been tasked with providing, writing, "I am cruelly limited to my actual experience of persons and things. ... Let me dry my eyes, and return to my narrative."[26] Even with Miss Clack and others commenting on their status as witnesses tasked with providing statements on their own experiences, *The Moonstone* still suits this category of casebook novels because there remains in its form that quality of miscellany earlier described resulting from the novel being multi-voice and multi-text. While not nearly as various in form as *The Woman in White*, *The Notting Hill Mystery*, and *Dracula*, *The Moonstone*'s documents include a family paper, witness narratives, journal extracts, letters, and statements.

Furthermore, while the majority of the novel is composed of narratives written by eyewitnesses after the events with the expressed purpose of serving as witnesses, some of the documents included were composed as private correspondence not authoritative testimony: the paper that opens the novel, which was intended for family reading; the letter from Mr. Candy to Blake, which details the death of Ezra Jennings; and the letter from Mr. Murthwaite addressed to Mr. Bruff, which ends the novel and tells of the diamond's reappearance in India. In Blake's narrative, he describes and records his reading of Rosanna Spearman's letter only to then stop out of "sincere distress" and hand it to Betteredge to read instead. What gets written down in Blake's narrative, then, is a "copy [of] the continuation of the letter from the original"[27] rather than a transcription of what Blake himself read in the moment because he refused to read. Here then are a few pages where the narrator breaks off contact with an authentic document in order to pass it to another character who does not narrate this section, and then at some later date copies down the remainder of the authentic document for the benefit of the reader. This odd moment of document engagement further emphasizes the pastiche quality of the novel. Additionally, because I want to focus primarily on the novelists' choice to compose these novels as documents and what that choice affords, I prefer to emphasize the material form of the novel in my terminology rather than the role of the character–writer.

Evidence and the Question of Truth

As multi-voice and multi-text casebooks, *The Woman in White*, *The Moonstone*, *The Notting Hill Mystery*, and *Dracula* present themselves as objective recordings of historical events, but their authenticity is undermined by the fact that they feature subjective, partial narratives and questionable remembrances of past events. As Lynn Pykett writes in *The Nineteenth-Century Sensation Novel*,

> The separate narratives are not only individual, they are also quite clearly idiosyncratic, subjective, quirky and partial. They are also limited; each particular narrator only knows part of the story, or, as in the case of *The Woman in White* and *The Moonstone*, is under strict instructions to confine him or herself to what he or she actually experienced. The result is a fragmentation of narrative and a dispersal of narrative authority. Instead of the utterance of the sagacious, omniscient narrator of the realist novel, we have a heap of fragments … .[28]

This raises questions, then, about the reliability of these fake documents. Can they be trusted? Do they convey a collective truth despite the possibility or even probability of human delusion or error? Furthermore, are documents even capable of *proving* anything?

The shrewd reader is not alone in asking these questions. The characters themselves sometimes admit to and describe the flaws in their writing, questioning their perceptions and judgments. In particular, they describe their inability to understand what is going on. In *Dracula*, Dr. John Seward reflects during his treatment of Lucy Westenra, "What does it all mean? I am beginning to wonder if my long habit of life amongst the insane is beginning to tell upon my own brain."[29] After

Walter's first encounter with Anne Catherick in *The Woman in White*, he writes, "I found myself doubting the reality of my own adventure ... I hardly knew where I was going, or what I meant to do next; I was conscious of nothing but the confusion of my own thoughts."[30] Later in the novel, Marian is bewildered by the way she failed to understand "the strength of Laura's unhappy attachment" to Walter, and she writes in her diary, "I have been sadly distrustful of myself ... The discovery that I have committed such an error in judgment as this, makes me hesitate about everything else."[31] And in *The Moonstone* the novel begins with "a family paper" that describes "The Storming of Seringapatam (1799)," the theft of a huge yellow diamond, and the reason why the document's author has "refuse[d] the right hand of friendship" to John Herncastle.[32] At the end of this family paper, the author, who has expressed a clear purpose in drafting the document, questions nearly everything he has put down on paper, using phrases like "Whether this be true or not,"[33] "I have no evidence but moral evidence,"[34] and "I have not only no proof that he killed the two men at the door; I cannot even declare that he killed the third man inside—for I cannot say that my own eyes saw the deed committed."[35] Ultimately, he decides to leave it to his readers, "our relatives, on either side," to "decide for themselves"[36] whether they believe that Herncastle murdered multiple men and stole the sacred diamond. Here, at the opening of this novel, the man who sets the story in motion and who has played the important role of documenting the diamond's origins, can only write down what he *believes to be true* and thus defends his decision to break off his relationship with his cousin, but he expresses that he lacks the evidence to say without a doubt that Herncastle deserves reprobation.

These brief examples illustrate that although these novels include pieces of evidence, the characters regularly find it difficult to provide readers and themselves with verifiable proof. Indeed, one could say that the difficulty of providing proof is the premise of these novels; these narratives relay again and again that pieces of evidence are inadequate in telling the whole story or conveying the truth. This does not necessarily mean that the various materials provided are insufficient as admissible testimony—indeed, they can be quite compelling and convincing—but rather it underscores the difficulties one encounters when trying to document acts of violence, greed, and malice. The villains of these novels (Dracula, Percival Glyde, Count Fosco, Baron R**, and Godfrey Ablewhite) do so much damage because they either go undetected for so long or because they possess powers that defy rational explanation. Glyde, Fosco, and Ablewhite astutely delude or privately control those around them in order to preserve their public reputations as decent men. The witnesses featured in *The Notting Hill Mystery* regularly comment on how kind Baron R** is to his wife, and they are baffled as to why she seems to dislike him. Dracula's ability to shapeshift defies logic. These villains significantly differ from each other, but they share a capacity to confound and elude.

A stirring example comes from *The Woman in White* in which one of the central, driving questions of the first half of the book is, "How can one know the true character of a man?" How can Marian, Laura, and Mr. Gilmore know if Sir Percival Glyde will be a good husband? Conversely, what becomes Walter's central concern following Laura's falsified death is, "How can one prove the terrible nature of a man?" In both cases, whether searching for virtue or vice, verifiable proof is difficult to come by. When Walter questions Marian about Sir Percival Glyde after Laura has received a troubling letter regarding him, he asks, "I suppose no whispers have ever been heard against his character?" Marian's reply reveals the challenges in evaluating a man's character when he benefits from the protective cover of a patriarchal society and the title of baronet:

> "Mr. Hartright! I hope you are not unjust enough to let that infamous letter influence you?"
>
> I felt the blood rush into my cheeks, for I knew that it *had* influenced me.
>
> "I hope not," I answered, confusedly. "Perhaps I had no right to ask the question."
>
> "I am not sorry you asked it," she said, "for it enables me to do justice to Sir Percival's reputation. Not a whisper, Mr. Hartright, has ever reached me, or my family, against him. He has fought successfully two contested elections; and has come out of the ordeal unscathed. A man who can do that, in England, is a man whose character is established."[37]

Marian's last sentence to Hartright is enough to make one squirm after learning of the depth of Glyde's depravity—lies, blackmail, domestic violence, debt, kidnapping, false imprisonment, forgery, and the theft of legitimacy and its accompanying inheritance. All this despite the fact that "[n]ot a whisper" has ever tainted Glyde's reputation; not even political opponents have suggested a proclivity to violence and control. Where is the evidence that Glyde has committed despicable acts? In the letter of a woman who was previously institutionalized? In the hazy memory of an abused wife? As the lawyer Mr. Kyrle tells Hartright, "[Y]ou have not the shadow of a case."[38] When Hartright sets out to find verifiable evidence of Glyde's crimes, the best he can hope for is locating proof of "a discrepancy between the date of the doctor's certificate and the date of Lady Glyde's journey to London."[39] Ultimately, what will give him a case are documents that contradict each other, that in their inconsistency show Lady Glyde could not have died when the testimonies of others say that she did. This means that Walter, Laura, and Marian's future depends upon an error that happens to be documented somewhere, somehow. It would be victory by means of negligence rather than positive identification.

When Hartright finally discovers Glyde's "Secret"—that he falsely claimed a baronetcy despite being an illegitimate heir—he does so by unearthing two documents that don't match: the original and copy marriage registries of Old Welmingham church. The explosive "Secret" alluded to throughout the novel with a capital letter, and guarded so defensively by Glyde, comes to light because of the fortuitous existence of a second copy of the marriage registry kept offsite in case anything were ever to happen to the original. While this moment of truth shocks Walter (and readers, too) by the "magnitude and daring of the crime that it represented," the truth Glyde died in order to protect also reveals the instability of documentary evidence. Documents are the source and remedy of fraud in this book. Through the marriage registry in the vestry Glyde commits his crime, and through the marriage registry in the offices of Robert Wansborough, Hartright discovers it. Even the book itself—a collection of documents from various characters—underscores the difficulty in presenting the whole truth in a narrative as one person's experiences will not do. It is the collective, with all its inconsistencies and contradictions, that gets closest to what really happened.

Adams's novel, *The Notting Hill Mystery*, on the other hand, explores the troubling possibility that one might not want to believe what the collective evidence suggests. From the narrative's first pages, Henderson confesses grave doubts about what his investigation on behalf of "the —— Life Assurance Association" has revealed. He pledges "accuracy and completeness" in his "minute and laborious investigation,"[40] but describes the result of such work unsatisfying because he cannot bring himself to believe the conclusion to which his evidence points. Henderson's task was to investigate the suspicious death of one "Madame R**," who died from drinking "a powerful acid … it is supposed, in her sleep," and whose husband held multiple insurance policies on her life totaling tens of thousands of pounds. Henderson collects and compiles "depositions" that suggest "Baron R**" is responsible for the deaths of three people through a combination of mesmerism, poisoning, and manipulation. The novel takes the form of a dossier or packet of materials Henderson mails to the insurance company in response to its request for an investigation. It includes letters, statements, journal entries, excerpts from periodicals, memoranda by Henderson that place events in context and reflect on findings, and a crime scene map that serves as the casebook's frontispiece. Despite the range of materials he collects pointing to the Baron's guilt, Henderson is unwilling unequivocally to endorse the possibility that Baron R** used mesmerism, and exploited "an extraordinary sympathy" between twin sisters to harm them and push Mr. Anderton to suicide. Henderson reflects,

> I have no hesitation in admitting that when the connection first suggested itself to my own mind, I at once dismissed it as too absurd to be entertained for a moment. But I feel bound to add, that the further my enquiries have progressed, the more strongly this apparent connection has forced itself upon me as the only clue to a maze of coincidences such as it has never before been my lot to encounter; and that while even now unable to accept it as a fact, I find it still more impossible to thrust it altogether on one side.[41]

In *The Woman in White*, Hartright finds it incredibly challenging to discover Glyde's "Secret" and prove that his wife's death was falsified (a task requiring extensive documentation), but Hartright fundamentally believes in Glyde's and Fosco's depravity. Their criminality does not challenge scientific law. Henderson, on the other hand, can neither ignore nor embrace what his evidence insinuates: that Baron R** used mesmerism to kill. He is stuck, and the language he uses to describe his conclusion on the case emphasizes the perplexing reality of his ambivalence. He "feel[s] bound" and has been "forced" to consider the "absurd." Completely flummoxed, Henderson refuses to rule on the case, instead passing that task to his employer and the other insurance companies who have to decide whether to pay out Baron R**'s policies. He writes,

> I am constrained to confess my own inability, after long and careful study, to decide. I have determined, therefore, simply to submit for your consideration the facts of the case as they appear in the depositions of the several parties from whom my information has been obtained.[42]

His use of "constrained," "inability," and "submit" underscores how hampered he feels despite the thoroughness of his investigation. Unable to take a definitive stance, Henderson closes the dossier, stating that his work is complete, but he can offer no other confident declaration:

> My task is done. In possession of the evidence thus placed before you, your judgment of its result will be as good as mine. Link by link you have now been put in possession of the entire chain. Is that chain one of purely accidental coincidences, or does it point with terrible certainty to a series of crimes, in their nature and execution almost too horrible to contemplate? That is the first question to be asked, and it is one to which I confess myself unable to reply. The second is more strange, and perhaps even more difficult still. Supposing the latter to be the case—are crimes thus committed susceptible of proof, or even if proved, are they of a kind for which the criminal can be brought to punishment?[43]

Not only has Henderson shirked the responsibility of providing a verdict, preferring that his employer come to a conclusion instead, but he has also closed the narrative with a perplexing question about justice. Cheryl Blake Price writes in her book *Chemical Crimes: Science and Poison in Victorian Crime Fiction* (2019) that "each [of Baron R**'s crimes] resists straightforward forensic legibility."[44] Henderson has tried to make these crimes legible through his gathering of evidence, but he can neither believe what he discovers nor imagine how one would prosecute such a case. Victorian novels, by and large, tend toward the comic, with happy endings that resolve major conflicts and offer fitting rewards and punishments. *The Notting Hill Mystery*, however, provides neither. The narrator cannot resolve his conflicting views about the case, and he does not believe the criminal could be brought to justice even if he were to make a claim against him.

In his thorough survey, *Crime Fiction since 1800: Detection, Death, Diversity* (2010), Stephen Knight claims that Collins's sensation novels offer

> consoling resolutions in sound moral responses, varying amounts of thoughtful detection and a great deal of well-organised and sometimes vertiginous plotting, as well as in masculinity that is, for the most part, clam and watchful—but very importantly also in female fidelity and endurance.[45]

Strikingly, Adams's novel does not provide "consoling resolutions in sound moral responses." At the end of the novel, it seems unlikely Baron R** will be brought to justice. In fact, unless the insurance companies choose to endorse mesmerism as the cause of Madame R**'s death, the baron will profit significantly from his actions, and he will escape a moral reckoning. Evidence pointing to Baron R**'s guilt does not ensure his prosecution, and it does not assure the chief investigator.

In *Dracula*, too, the notion of proof through evidence is precarious. The novel contains a vast number of documents, including journal entries, letters (opened and unopened), telegrams, memoranda, notes, and newspaper clippings logged in different recording methods: longhand, shorthand, phonograph recording, and typewriting. Like the material elements of Collins's and Adams's novels, these documents purportedly provide readers with an objective view of the case. Despite how the

documents have corroborated important details and have provided plenty
of eyewitness testimony, Jonathan writes in his note that closes the novel,

> In the summer of this year we made a journey to Transylvania,
> and went over the old ground which was, and is, to us so full of
> vivid and terrible memories. It was almost impossible to believe
> that the things which we had seen with our own eyes and heard
> with our own ears were living truths. Every trace of all that had
> been was blotted out. The castle stood as before, reared high
> above a waste of desolation.
>
> When we got home we got to talking of the old time ... I
> took the papers from the safe where they have been ever since our
> return so long ago. We were struck with the fact that, in all the
> mass of material of which the record is composed, there is hardly
> one authentic document! nothing but a mass of type-writing,
> except the later note-books of Mina and Seward and myself, and
> Van Helsing's memorandum. We could hardly ask anyone, even
> did we wish to, to accept these as proofs of so wild a story.[46]

Jonathan's closing comments acknowledge the difficulty of believing what
they had experienced even for themselves, and he observes that "in all the
mass of material ... there is hardly one authentic document." Despite the
evidence of their eyes, their memories, and their narratives, Jonathan, like
Henderson, cannot imagine asking anyone to believe what the documents
contain.

It is a central irony of these works, then, that while they include
documents that supposedly verify the contents within, the stories they
tell dwell on the difficulty of proving such extraordinary circumstances
and characters. Collins, Adams, and Stoker knowingly embed this irony
in their novels, which, importantly in thrillers, destabilizes the reader's
trust in verifiable proof. The books rely heavily upon readers' appetite for
clarity, but their fragmented, multi-voice and multi-text nature undercut
the notion that truth is knowable or easily documentable. The fictional
editors of these Victorian casebook novels catalog the evidence of a case,
but their records regularly emphasize the limitations of human knowledge and the documentability of human experience. Truth, even at its

seemingly most plain, is difficult to come by, tricky to verify, challenging to accept, and investigated by an interested (and, even in Collins's novels, financially invested) party.

Each of these novels *builds a case*, whether it be to restore an identity (*The Woman in White*), release someone from suspicion (*The Moonstone*), investigate insurance fraud (*The Notting Hill Mystery*), or record the heroic efforts of a brave group battling a terrifying monster (*Dracula*). They are thus clearly interested in the truth. But while these casebooks claim impartiality and critical distance, they are in fact a biased collection of documents. They have an expressed purpose that the editor pursues in his or her organization and selection of the materials. Can we trust collections of documents that editors claim are objective but upon close reading are observably partisan, that are devoted to securing the interests of one party?

For example, Collins's *The Woman in White* was first serialized weekly in Charles Dickens's *All the Year Round*, from November 26, 1859, to August 25, 1860, and begins with a "Preamble" describing the composition and purpose of the documents that follow.[47] Written by Walter Hartright, it begins by commenting on the legal system's inadequacy and thus the need to present these materials:

> This is the story of what a Woman's patience can endure, and what a Man's resolution can achieve.
>
> If the machinery of the Law could be depended on to fathom every case of suspicion, and to conduct every process of inquiry, with moderate assistance only from the lubricating influences of oil and gold, the events which fill these pages might have claimed their share of the public attention in a Court of Justice.
>
> But the Law is still, in certain inevitable cases, the pre-engaged servant of the long purse; and the story is left to be told, for the first time, in this place. As the Judge might once have heard it, so the Reader shall hear it now. No circumstance of importance, from the beginning to the end of the disclosure, shall be related on hearsay evidence. When the writer of these introductory lines (Walter Hartright by name) happens to be more closely connected than others with the incidents to be recorded,

he will describe them in his own person. When his experience fails, he will retire from the position of narrator; and his task will be continued, from the point at which he has left it off, by other persons who can speak to the circumstances under notice from their own knowledge, just as clearly and positively as he has spoken before them.

Thus, the story here presented will be told by more than one pen, as the story of an offence against the laws is told in Court by more than one witness—with the same object, in both cases, to present the truth always in its most direct and most intelligible aspect; and to trace the course of one complete series of events, by making the persons who have been most closely connected with them, at each successive stage, relate their own experience, word for word.

Let Walter Hartright, teacher of drawing, aged twenty-eight years, be heard first.[48]

These four paragraphs effectively introduce the novel and its structure to readers, and they emphasize the care with which the documents have been selected and arranged. The tone is measured and purposeful and communicates Hartright's diligent work in bringing together a great deal of evidence to tell a story that has been ignored by "the machinery of the Law." Despite the fact that his work has occurred outside of a court of law, he uses language and phrasing that is official and even bureaucratic. He speaks of "incidents," "to conduct every process of inquiry," "disclosure," "hearsay evidence," "in his own person," "persons who can speak to the circumstances under notice," and "an offence against the laws." Hartright intentionally presents himself as a neutral arbiter seeking to gain the trust of his readers. He claims that "the Law is still, in certain inevitable cases, the pre-engaged servant of the long purse," thus necessitating this disclosure of "the story" by those directly involved in the proceedings. His purpose is to address this gap in the law's ability to expose wrongdoing and deliver justice in the case of Laura Fairlie, Anne Catherick, Count Fosco, and Percival Glyde.[49] Hartright uses legal language not only because of Percival's despicable behavior and crime, but also because he wants to establish that the casebook before readers' eyes is theirs to evaluate: "As the Judge might once have heard it, so the Reader shall hear it now."

While we may consider this "Preamble" straightforward at first glance, Hartright's position and purpose are more complicated than he admits. He claims to provide the reader with "the truth always in its most direct and most intelligible aspect ... by making the persons who have been most closely connected with them ... relate their own experience, word for word." Noble enough, it seems, but by casting readers as "Judge," and claiming simply to be a conveyor of information, he distances himself from the curation of the included materials. While proclaiming himself as the editor of the casebook, he also seeks to detach himself from any insinuation of partiality. When a reader encounters these claims at the beginning of the novel, she will likely not think anything of them. But once she has completed the book and seen Hartright's vested financial interest in the restoration of Laura's true identity she may wonder whether Hartright is truly as neutral as he presents himself in those early pages.

Far from being neutral, Hartright has a clearly expressed purpose. Despite the fact that the lawyer Mr. Kyrle tells him, "Mr. Hartright ... you have not the shadow of a case"[50] and "there is no case, Mr. Hartright— there is really no case," Hartright seeks to build one.[51] He tells Mr. Kyrle,

> [Lady Glyde] has been cast out as a stranger from the house in which she was born—a lie which records her death has been written on her mother's tomb—and there are two men, alive and unpunished, who are responsible for it. That house shall open again to receive her, in the presence of every soul who followed the false funeral to the grave; that lie shall be publicly erased from the tombstone, by the authority of the head of the family; and those two men shall answer for their crime to ME."[52]

The documents Hartright collects and presents are supposedly the result of his effort to make these men answer for their crimes. Walter M. Kendrick calls this "Hartright's campaign of textual renovation."[53] Despite his romantic and financial interest in the outcome of the case, Hartright seeks the trust of his audience, claiming that he is not motivated to help Laura by

any "base speculation on the future relations" between the two of them—
that is, any idea that his helping her will advance their relationship.[54]

The Moonstone, too, has an expressed purpose. Gabriel Betteredge
describes this objective at the beginning of his narrative by recording
Franklin Blake's request of him:

> "Betteredge," says Mr. Franklin, "I have been to the lawyer's about
> some family matters; and, among other things, we have been
> talking of the loss of the Indian Diamond, in my aunt's house in
> Yorkshire, two years since. Mr Bruff thinks as I think, that the
> whole story ought, in the interests of truth, to be placed on record
> in writing—and the sooner the better."[55]

He goes on to say that "the characters of innocent people have suffered
under suspicion already—as you know. The memories of innocent people
may suffer, hereafter, for want of a record of the facts to which those
who come after us can appeal." While Blake, the compiler of these documents, does not explicitly recruit his audience to play the role of judge
the way Hartright does at the beginning of *The Woman in White*, the
premise of requesting these narratives remains a supposedly legal one
as Blake has consulted with a lawyer and "Mr Bruff and I together have
hit on the right way of telling it."[56] The language he uses to justify this
action is also legalistic as he wants the story "in the interest of truth, to
be placed on record in writing." He and Betteredge discuss "a record of
the facts," "certain events," "certain persons concerned in those events,"
and "an old family paper, which relates the necessary particulars on the
authority of an eye-witness."[57] Similar to the bureaucratic language with
which Hartright begins *The Woman in White*, Blake's request for testimo-
nials "in the interest of truth" seems honorable, earnest, and impartial.
And, like Hartright, we discover later Blake too has a vested interest in this
endeavor because although he does not explicitly say so at the start of the
novel it is his good name that has been questioned. The collection's service
to the monetary and romantic interests of the lead male character negates
the worthiness of his pursuits. Rather, it underscores a key affordance of
casebook writing: these documents are seemingly objective and wholistic

in their scope and yet are highly subjective and limited in their perspective at the same time. For a mystery writer like Collins, this significantly advantages him in blinding readers to certain information and drawing them on to invest in certain narratives and perspectives more than others.

One way that Collins does this in *The Moonstone* is by having his narrators remind readers regularly of the purpose and scope of their writing. In doing so, he craftily reminds his audience of the grounding, documentary conceit of this book (that these are authentic documents written by the people involved) and this continues to make readers believe throughout that they possess intimate knowledge of the case. This is in spite of the fact that the collection of first-person narratives actually significantly limits our knowledge of the case and all its contours. Furthermore, the character-narrators discuss their limited knowledge and capability openly and use their expressions about their limitations to bolster their credibility. Betteredge, the narrator of the largest chunk of the book, tells readers at the end of his first narrative,

> In the dark, I have brought you thus far. In the dark I am compelled to leave you, with my best respects.
>
> Why compelled? it may be asked. Why not take the persons who have gone along with me, so far, up into those regions of superior enlightenment in which I sit myself?
>
> In answer to this, I can only state that I am acting under orders, and that those orders have been given to me (as I understand) in the interests of truth. I am forbidden to tell more in this narrative than I knew myself at the time. Or, to put it plainer, I am to keep strictly within the limits of my own experience, and am not to inform you of what other persons told me—for the very sufficient reason that you are to have the information from those other persons themselves, at first hand. In this matter of the Moonstone the plan is, not to present reports, but to produce witnesses. I picture to myself a member of the family reading these pages fifty years hence. Lord! what a compliment he will feel it, to be asked to take nothing on hearsay, and to be treated in all respects like a Judge on the bench.[58]

Betteredge's repetition of the collection's purpose serves to enhance the credibility of his contribution by highlighting that the loyal servant could say more but does not "in the interests of truth." He writes only of what he experienced directly, and his reminder to readers of the book's intentions reinforces the idea that they are provided objective accounts and are not being duped along the way but honestly lead forward in solving the case. Collins plants one of these reminders in Drusilla Clack's narrative, too, when Clack breaks from her narrative to include correspondence between herself and Blake in which she attempts to evangelize to him. She writes informing him that "attached to her own manuscript" she has included "copious Extracts from precious publications in her possession, all bearing on this terrible subject" and wishing that "those Extracts (Miss Clack fervently hopes) sound as the blast of a trumpet in the ears of her respected kinsman, Mr Franklin Blake."[59] The correspondence between Blake and Clack she includes in her narrative show perfectly in miniature how Collins can utilize these forms to his advantage. First, Blake's denial of her request to give more information than she's been asked to provide reminds readers of the supposed purpose and format of the book as a whole. In particular, Blake's reminder to Clack that she "limit herself to her own individual experience of persons and events, as recorded in her diary" and "Later discoveries she will be good enough to leave to the pens of those persons who can write in the capacity of actual witnesses."[60] Blake's refusal reminds readers that they are supposedly getting the truth from each of these narrators because they are directed explicitly and even corrected when they veer away from their purpose. This builds trust in Blake as a shrewd editor, but it also works to persuade readers that they are getting intimate access to important information. Clack's back and forth with Blake comes near the end of her narrative when readers have already become well acquainted with her delusions about Godfrey Ablewhite and her passion but ineptitude as an evangelist. Clack and the other narrators of The Moonstone emphasize (even if unintentionally at times) the importance of keeping focused on the task at hand so that readers find comfort in the sense that they are getting an honest picture of characters and events. Pykett calls this "an impression of verisimilitude or actuality."[61] These moments when characters discuss their strict instructions and limitations assure readers that they are in good hands—the rules are being followed—but this faithful adherence to the rules obscures, to Collins's benefit, how narrow our view is of the big picture. Even so, the Victorian and contemporary reader are never in doubt as to the supposed purpose of this multi-voice, multi-text book since the character-narrators comment on it directly.

Dracula, more than in Collins's novels, chronicles the process of assembling the casebook for a specific purpose. While Hartright's "Preamble" casts readers as Judge in *The Woman in White*, the gathering of materials is done silently, offstage. Readers simply receive the materials without knowing for the most part how they were commissioned, gathered, and arranged. In *Dracula*, though, the creation, arranging, and sharing of the documents is part of the plot. A short note before chapter 1 reads, "How these papers have been placed in sequence will be made clear in the reading of them."[62] They are not merely collected after the fact in order to make record of an event; in Stoker's novel the documents themselves (a staggering variety of materials) help the characters understand what is going on.

Despite this kind of "behind the scenes" access to the narrative's creation, the casebook's relation to verifiable, objective truth remains strained. Collins's and Adams's novels relay an attempt to capture truth post hoc, but Stoker's *Dracula* displays how challenging it is to even understand what is happening *in the present moment*. Mina believes that she and her companions can better understand the strange course of events each has encountered separately if they share documents and create a chronological record of them. After Jonathan's mental health takes a turn for the worse when he sees a younger-looking Count Dracula in the streets of London, Mina reads her husband's journal to try and understand the cause of Jonathan's distress. Having read its horrors, Mina writes in her journal,

> There seems to be through it all some thread of continuity .... That fearful Count was coming to London, with its teeming millions. ... There may be a solemn duty; and if it come we must not shrink from it. ... I shall be prepared. I shall get my typewriter this very hour and begin transcribing. Then we shall be ready for other eyes if required.[63]

Jonathan's journal is the document that begins Stoker's novel. Here, about halfway through the novel, Mina is telling us how it came to be before our eyes, how it came to be transcribed "for other eyes." The other eyes with whom Mina first shares the transcribed journal are those of Dr. Van Helsing, whom Mina hopes can help care for Jonathan and somehow explain or validate the disturbing contents of Jonathan's journal. Her sharing of this transcript with Van Helsing serves to cement his respect for her and her husband ("He is a noble fellow" and "I am dazzle—dazzle more than ever") and to recuperate Jonathan. Van Helsing's validating proclamation that Jonathan's experiences, although "Strange and terrible," are "true,"[64] makes him turn into "a new man."[65] Thus, while in Collins's and Adams's novels the documents are supposedly collected in order to persuade and inform an outside audience, in the case of *Dracula* they are collected to aid the group in defeating the vampire and saving Mina from a terrible fate. The recording and sharing of Jonathan's writing helps revive his physical and mental fortitude, the transcription of Seward's diary helps them recognize connections between Renfield's behavior and the Count's actions, and a variety of documents help them understand the vampire's abilities and limitations.[66]

On the one hand, we could say that *Dracula* then demonstrates the epistemological power of collaboration. Stoker lays plain the near impossibility of understanding a violent and existential threat in the moment, but the group comes to understand the threat they face by pooling their material and intellectual resources. Mina tells Seward at one point, "because in the struggle which we have before us to rid the earth of this terrible monster we must have all the knowledge and all the help which we can get."[67] They succeed in their mission because the documents help them connect threads and predict the vampire's next pursuits. This happy ending, though, does not erase the pages of confusion, fraught disbelief, and panicked questioning. Nor does it assuage the fear that without this incredible, collaborative effort the vampire would have continued on his bloody rampage. In the case of *Dracula*, one doctor is not enough. One highly skilled and intuitive woman is not enough. One type of material evidence is not enough. Only through collaborating intimately and intentionally, stringing fragments of text and experiences together, can the group successfully challenge the monster. And even then, what Johnathan says at the end is that no one could possibly consider what they documented as verifiable.

What all this points to is a subgenre that revels in—even relies upon—a shifty and splintered presentation of truth. For a kind of writing often described as conservative or comforting, perhaps this is surprising. Stephen Knight describes crime fiction as texts in which "[s]pecially skilled people discover the cause of a crime, restore order and bring the criminal to account."[68] With the notable exception of *The Notting Hill Mystery*, Knight's claim holds true for the casebook novels I have discussed here. *The Moonstone, The Woman in White*, and *Dracula* all resolve satisfactorily—that is, the heroes are rewarded, and the villains are punished. Order is restored, and the cases (and their books) can be closed. These casebook novels repeatedly show, however, the difficulty of achieving that closure when faced with horrifying acts of greed, violence, and manipulation. So, while the casebook form of these novels undoubtedly contributes to their suspense and the reader's pleasure in reading them, the form also exposes disturbing cracks in our confidence of what can be represented on paper. And while three of the four novels discussed here end with consoling moral judgments, these casebooks can be construed as a criticism of the idea that evidence is a reliable arbiter of knowledge and justice.

I have to wonder, then, if this contributes to the continued reverence for and interest in these documentary novels. While scholars have tended to focus on the limitations rather than affordances of epistolary writing, for example, they have treated casebook novels and their unique narrative limitations with significantly more appreciation and awareness of their benefits. In large part this is because first-person documents perfectly suit casebook novels in which there is a crime, scandal, secret, or threat that the author wishes to conceal and use to lure the reader. The restrictions that first-person, document-bound narration entails significantly aids the novelist in crafting narratives in which suspense builds, an ensemble cast gets fleshed out,[69] and the reader latches onto clues and yet remains ignorant as to the full truth or scope of the case. Close attention to the form of these Victorian casebook novels also reveals how the fragmented narratives, competing ideas, gaps, and confusion of the characters themselves suggest an inadequacy of individual knowledge, experience, and documentation. Perhaps this, too, is why these books continue to fascinate in a post-truth, post-modern world.

Conclusion

One joy of working on this book has been getting reading recommendations from people. When folks would ask what this book is about and I would say it is about novels written as documents like letters, diaries, travel journals, and so on, people would often respond, "Oh! You mean like _____?" Many times they would name a novel published in the last few years, and it made clear to me time and again that documentary novels are alive and well in the twenty-first century. Even the much-maligned epistolary novel, supposedly dead after 1800, proves to be among the living, with popular and critically acclaimed novels published just in my time writing this book, including Anne Youngson's *Meet Me at the Museum* (2018), Claire Fuller's *Swimming Lessons* (2018), and Veera Hiranandani's juvenile novel *The Night Diary* (2018), a creative blend of diary and letter writing, which earned the prestigious Newbery Honor in 2019. Margaret Atwood's greatly anticipated sequel to her powerful documentary novel *The Handmaid's Tale* (1985) was published in 2019. *The Testaments* features the testimonies of three women whose collective narration tells the story of Gilead's rise and fall. The novel won the Man Booker Prize.

Early in this book I proposed using a family tree model of literary history rather than a timeline, and I hope that other researchers will recognize the utility of this schema and build upon it. Certainly the books of Youngson, Fuller, Hiranandani, and Atwood have earned a place on the tree, and work could be done to connect these modern-day documentary novels to their ancestors in the British canon. I hope other scholars will makes these connections, fitting their analyses into my framework or pushing against it in productive and compelling ways. I am confident that readers will find notable exceptions to the rules I have laid out here, but my certainty of that fact only makes me more committed to the model of a literary family tree. Families are messy. They contain strained relationships as well as harmonious ones, legitimate heirs and unacknowledged offspring, places of continuation and breakdown, golden children and black sheep. So, too, can a literary family tree show points of connection, disintegration, resemblance, conflict, germination, growth, groupings, outliers, and repetition. In short, a tree model allows for complexity, and those of us who read, teach, and research novels know that these books are wonderfully complex.

Historians and theoreticians of the novel have suggested at times that documentary novels lack the complexity of narratives with a third-person point of view—particularly those that use free indirect discourse. For example, Dorrit Cohn writes, "In sum, the narrated monologue [Cohn's term for free indirect discourse] is at once a more complex and a more flexible technique for rendering consciousness than the rival techniques."[1] After having spent the past few years immersed in documentary novels of the last three hundred years, I am convinced more than ever of the narrowness of that perspective. While writing through fake documents is a significantly limiting form, to suggest that fictional narratives that do not feature free indirect style or an omniscient narrator lack psychological depth ignores the ways novelists can exploit the potentialities of the first-person documentary narrative.

I can think of no novel that better illustrates this point on the British side of the family tree than *The Remains of the Day* (1989) by Nobel Laureate Kazuo Ishiguro. His novel, which won the Man Booker Prize, challenges Cohn's claim and represents the kind of creativity within constraints I have discussed in each chapter of this book. As such, *The Remains of the Day* occupies a branch on the family tree of documentary novels. It is an illustrious descendant of its Victorian ancestors and reminds us that this form, with roots going back to the first novels in English, remains vibrant. Ishiguro's chief achievement in the novel is his masterful use of the first person and all its limitations. Mr. Stevens, an aging butler in a grand old English house, takes a motoring trip to see a former colleague, and he writes about this journey and his remembrances of working under his former employer, Lord Darlington. The novel takes the form of a travel memoir as Stevens moves back and forth between his current journey to see Miss Kenton and his reflections on key life moments that have impacted his understanding of greatness within his profession. The constraints that this form places on Ishiguro are significant: he is limited to writing from Stevens's point of view, a man who has hardly left the grounds of Darlington Hall over the course of many decades.

Even so, Ishiguro manages to create a multifaceted narrative that is both linear and not linear at all. It is linear in the sense that it begins with Stevens setting out on a journey that he does take.[2] It is not linear at all, however, in the sense that Stevens's recollections of past events do not move in a strict chronological pattern. The linear plotting of Stevens leaving Darlington Hall to meet Miss Kenton exists alongside the butler's memories that he sometimes places correctly in terms of timing and sometimes fails to recollect with accuracy. The resulting tension between Stevens's present and past, particularly his self-curtailed perspective on that past, creates a potent narrative of a human's inability to fully comprehend himself or the world around him until it is too late.

The reader ultimately discovers that the novel's limited point of view and Stevens's memory gaps are central to the book's exploration of self-delusion. Stevens has devoted his life to Lord Darlington, who, the reader comes to recognize before Stevens does, is a Nazi sympathizer. Ishiguro's carefully wrought prose simultaneously captures Stevens's strict adherence to the decorum and demands of his profession while also revealing the human cost of that devotion, which Stevens hardly recognizes. The writer–protagonist's reflections reveal more to the reader than the butler sees or understands himself. Stevens considers his greatest accomplishment as a butler, for example, to be the devotion and restraint he showed during the consequential "conference of 1923."[3] This gathering of distinguished guests demands that Stevens not only expertly manage the house and his large staff in preparation of a logistically challenging event, but also that he accommodate requests from his superiors as varied as informing a young man about "the facts of life" (sexual intercourse), assisting guests who arrive days earlier than expected, and responding to the "snapping ... fingers" of a French gentleman with sores on his feet who "every few hours" requests bandages and medical attention.[4] Stevens performs these duties with great devotion to his employer while exerting himself extraordinarily. For while Stevens refills glasses of port, instructs staff, and retains his formal, steadfast bearing, his seventy-two-year-old father lies dying upstairs. After learning that his father has likely had a stroke, Stevens makes his way around the room pouring drinks until one guest says to him,

> "Stevens, are you all right?"
> "Yes, sir. Perfectly."
> "You look as though you're crying."
> I laughed and taking out a handkerchief, quickly wiped my face.
> "I'm very sorry, sir. The strains of a hard day."[5]

Just a moment later, the consummate butler learns his father has died. Reflecting on his work that night, Stevens states, "For all its sad associations, whenever I recall that evening today, I find I do so with a large sense of triumph."[6] The butler who is a paragon of restraint uses the word *triumph* to describe his exertions that night. The only indication we have that the experience has been incredibly trying is Mr. Cardinal's observation that the butler stands there crying. He does not notice—or he refuses to acknowledge—the tears streaming down his own face. Kathleen Wall describes the self-restraint Stevens and his father exhibit in the novel as "a denial of personal feelings so extreme as to be disturbing."[7] Crucially, we register this emotional disturbance, but Stevens does not. Ishiguro masterfully exploits the gap between what we know Stevens should see, understand, or do, and what Stevens is capable of allowing himself to see, understand, or do. That gap, that slippage, is what suffuses the novel with such poignancy—an emotional resonance made possible by the novel's constrained documentary form and limited point of view.

The form of the novel as a written recording of Stevens's reflections only further solidifies this fissure between what the butler should recognize but cannot. Wall writes,

The issue of unreliability thus saturates both form and content, making this novel an ideal vehicle for exploring, more methodically and in more detail, how narrative unreliability is communicated and what devices the implied author has at his disposal for constructing two contradictory voices that we hear simultaneously.[8]

Ishiguro's chosen narrative vehicle constrains itself to the written reflections of a man especially skilled at denying his own needs and desires. Stevens cannot see the truth of Darlington's slip into moral corruption, and he cannot understand the truth of his own role in it. Ishiguro's novel powerfully reminds us that what we think about ourselves and what we even commit to paper about ourselves may not be true.

The reality of this is heart wrenching. Only at one moment, when Stevens sits next to a stranger at the end of the novel, does the aging butler recognize and communicate what he has sacrificed: "All those years I served him, I trusted I was doing something worthwhile. I can't even say I made my own mistakes. Really—one has to ask oneself—what dignity is there in that?"[9] Salman Rushdie describes Stevens here as "a man destroyed by the ideas upon which he has built his life."[10] Because Ishiguro utilized the incredibly constraining premise of a man documenting his thoughts on what it means to be a "great butler," a goal requiring the surrender of a person's individuality, the novel perfectly conveys the psychological burden of such a life.[11] In other words, the constraints of a first-person documentary novel and Ishiguro's ingenious use of its affordances generates a text of immense complexity that negates Cohn's summation that first-person narratives cannot rival free indirect discourse in rendering human consciousness.

So why does Ishiguro's achievement matter? What is important about the narrative creativity and resourcefulness of any novel discussed in this book? Recognizing and appreciating brilliant work within constraining forms has important pedagogical and political implications. As students read and interrogate these kinds of texts, they begin to recognize these writers' amazing accomplishments within significant constraints. In doing so, students hone skills that in their careers—as writers, teachers, marketing professionals, attorneys, social workers, politicians, museum curators, HR specialists, clergy, law enforcement officials, scientists, engineers, and CEOs —will help them be creative, imaginative, and boundary-pushing while facing the constraints that exist in *all* of those careers. One of the perennial challenges we face in the humanities is the toxic idea that studying books is not particularly valuable or important. But what we do in every class is push students to think within and beyond constraints, to be inventive even when it seems like there is not any room for creativity, and to refine their ability to see beauty and originality. These are skills that transcend any disciplinary boundary, any career path—they are quite simply the skills necessary to navigate and thrive in our complex world. Documentary novels and the ways their authors test the limitations and affordances of their form are instructive materials in our mission to advance our students' critical and creative thinking abilities.

In the political arena, we live in a world in which barriers to equitable education, healthcare, natural resources, and food circumscribe vast numbers of people to substandard and even inexcusable living conditions. We desperately need creative solutions to seemingly intractable problems—that is, seemingly permanent forms of social hierarchies, economic classes, racial constructions, and legal systems. Caroline Levine writes at the end of her article "Not Against Structure, but in Search of Better Structures,"

> I am trying to bring into the field of our formalist analysis the many nonaesthetic forms—orders and arrangements of space and resources that include congressional districts and sewage systems—that structure the polis. These are the forms that urgently need to be understood as designs and arrangements that can be reshaped, reorganized, and redistributed. In this sense, they are no different from aesthetic objects: they are artifices that take many shapes, and they can be both made and remade.[12]

This is not mere optimism. It is a reminder that all forms can be transfigured and that our literary history is full of remarkable examples to which we can turn for inspiration and guidance. Documentary novels as a corpus illustrate the human capacity to push against ostensibly unmovable constraints. Seeing them as innovative helps us better imagine new ways forward despite the obstacles we face. As Ishiguro expressed in his Nobel lecture in 2017, "Good writing and good reading will break down barriers. We may even find a new idea, a great humane vision, around which to rally."[13] The history of the novel, if nothing else, is a fascinating account of human experimentation, and documentary novels are a compelling sampling that underscores the wondrous possibilities of fiction and the tremendous capacities of the human mind.

Notes

Introduction

1   George Eliot, *Adam Bede* (London: Penguin, 2008), 197, 193. I've used the gender neutral "themselves" here to refer to Eliot's narrator. Claire Harman notes that the "Autobiography" subtitle of *Jane Eyre* was first suggested by Brontë's publisher. The young author

> accepted the firm's other suggestion that the title could be changed, and "Jane Eyre: a novel in three vols. By Currer Bell" became "Jane Eyre: An Autobiography. Edited by Currer Bell." Someone at Smith, Elder … had recognised the potential of making readers wonder—could this story actually *be true*? The tweak to the title created a fiction that made the heroine Jane less fictional, made her into an autobiographer, "edited"—at some distance in time … by Currer Bell.

> Claire Harman, *Charlotte Brontë: A Fiery Heart* (New York: Alfred A. Knopf, 2016), 256–57.

2   Lennard J. Davis, *Factual Fictions: The Origins of the English Novel* (New York: Columbia University Press, 1983), 35.

3   Doug Underwood, *Journalism and the Novel: Truth and Fiction, 1700–2000* (Cambridge: Cambridge University Press, 2011), 34.

4   Michael McKeon, *The Origins of the English Novel, 1600–1740* (Baltimore, MD: Johns Hopkins University Press, 1987), 35; E. L. Doctorow, *E.L. Doctorow, Essays and Conversations* (Princeton, NJ: Ontario Review Press, 1982), 21.

5   Underwood, *Journalism and the Novel*, 35.

6   Aphra Behn, *Oroonoko: or the Royal Slave. A True History* (London: Printed for Will. Canning, 1688), unpag.

7   Brett C. McInelly, "Expanding Empires, Expanding Selves: Colonialism, the Novel, and 'Robinson Crusoe,'" *Studies in the Novel* 35, no. 1 (2003): 3.

8   Davis, *Factual Fictions*, 133.

9   Bertil Romberg, *Studies in the Narrative Technique of the First-Person Novel* (Stockholm: Almqvist & Wiksell, 1962), 69.

10   Davis, *Factual Fictions*, 16.

11   Virginia Woolf, *The Common Reader, Second Series* (London: Hogarth Press, 1932), unpag.

12   Daniel Defoe, *Robinson Crusoe*, ed. Tom Keymer (Oxford: Oxford University Press, 2008), 43.

13   Malinda Snow has argued convincingly that scientific writing in particular influenced Defoe's style. She writes,

> But what stimulated Defoe's ability to write convincing narrative? In what works had he seen not only a skillful use of the simple, idiomatic style of daily speech and the ready talent for objective description but also the unifying presence of a first-person narrator who describes himself and his activities? He saw all these in scientific writing. The tone of later seventeenth-century scientists is quite unlike that of modern scientific writing. It is more chatty and intimate, with frequent personal references, asides, and even occasional religious ejaculations. One hears the unmistakable voice of an individual whose presence unifies a series of experiments and discoveries. In short, these works share characteristics that are also central to Defoe's fiction and to the rise of the novel.

Malinda Snow, "The Origins of Defoe's First-Person Narrative Technique: An Overlooked Aspect of the Rise of the Novel," *Journal of Narrative Technique* 6, no. 3 (1976): 176.

14   Samuel Richardson, *Clarissa, or, The History of a Young Lady*, ed. Angus Ross (New York: Penguin), 37.

15   Richardson, *Clarissa*, 36.

16   John Richetti, "Introduction," *The Cambridge Companion to the Eighteenth-Century Novel* (Cambridge: Cambridge University Press, 1996), 1.

17   Joe Bray, *The Epistolary Novel: Representations of Consciousness* (London: Routledge, 2003), 1. Bray also argues that scholars have emphasized "the epistolary novel's perceived inferiority in a key area of the novel's responsibilities: the representation of consciousness. From its beginnings, the novel has been associated with some kind of an attempt to render individual psychology, to delve into the minds of its characters. The epistolary novel is often thought to present a relatively unsophisticated and transparent version of subjectivity, as its letter-writers apparently jot down

whatever is passing through their heads at the moment of writing" (1). Bray, however, challenges this idea by attempting to demonstrate that in the epistolary novel "Thoughts and feelings are not as unmediated and transparent in the fictional letter as has often been supposed. Rather, epistolary novelists such as Richardson explore with great subtlety complex tensions within the divided minds of their characters. As a result, the way the epistolary novel represents consciousness has significant consequences for the history of third-person narrative, beyond the date of its apparent demise" (2).

18 Ian Watt, *The Rise of the Novel: Studies in Defoe, Richardson, and Fielding* (Berkeley: University of California Press, 1957), 210. While Watt enumerates the challenges of the epistolary form, in chapter 7 he also emphasizes Samuel Richardson's skill in using "a great variety of auxiliary devices" to navigate these difficulties in *Clarissa*.

19 Watt, *Rise of the Novel*, 297. Elaine McGirr, too, describes free indirect discourse as "a popular and largely successful solution to the problems of interpretation, authority, and believability" in epistolary novels and recognizes this technique as being "best employed in Jane Austen's novels." Elaine McGirr, "Interiorities," in *The Cambridge History of the English Novel*, ed. Robert Caserio and Clement Hawes (Cambridge: Cambridge University Press, 2012), 93.

20 Mary A. Favret, *Romantic Correspondence: Women, Politics and the Fiction of Letters* (Cambridge: Cambridge University Press, 1993), 145.

21 Dinah Birch, "Epistolary Novel," in *The Oxford Companion to English Literature*, 7th ed. (Oxford: Oxford University Press, 2009). See also *Encyclopedia of Life Writing: Autobiographical and Biographical Forms*, ed. Margaretta Jolly (London: Routledge, 2001), which describes epistolary fiction as experiencing a "relative eclipse, from the mid-19th to the mid-20th century"; *The Cambridge Guide to Women's Writing in English*, ed. Lorna Sage (Cambridge: Cambridge University Press, 1999), which describes epistolary novels as having been "at their most popular during the 18th century" and having "played an important part in the 'rise' and wider definition of the novel"; *Britannica Concise Encyclopedia* (Chicago: Encyclopædia Britannica, Inc., 2006), which describes it as "the forerunner of the modern psychological novel" and "popular up to the 19th century"; and *Oxford Bibliographies* (www.oxfordbibliographies.com/), which describes its decrease in popularity as an "*abrupt withering* of the genre at the turn of the 19th century" (emphasis added).

22 Wayne B. Booth, *The Rhetoric of Fiction*, 2nd ed. (Harmondsworth: Penguin Books, 1991), 153.

23 George Levine, *How to Read the Victorian Novel* (Oxford: Wiley-Blackwell, 2007), 3.

24 Booth, *Rhetoric of Fiction*, 136.

25 Alexandra Valint, *Narrative Bonds: Multiple Narrators in the Victorian Novel* (Columbus: Ohio State University Press, 2021), 44–45.

26 Audrey Jaffe claims "Realism in this book is thus not fantasy's alternative, as the usual generic distinctions would have it, but rather its fulfillment." Audrey Jaffe, *The Victorian Novel Dreams of the Real: Conventions and Ideology* (New York: Oxford University Press, 2016), 5.

27 Booth, *Rhetoric of Fiction*, 27.

28 Booth, *Rhetoric of Fiction*, 59.

29 Lilian R. Furst, *All Is True: The Claims and Strategies of Realist Fiction* (Durham, NC: Duke University Press, 1995), 10.

30 James Wood, *How Fiction Works* (London: Jonathan Cape, 2008), 83.

31 Furst, *All Is True*, 26.

32 Furst, *All Is True*, 47.

33 Underwood, *Journalism and the Novel*, 3.

34 Mas'ud Zavarzadeh, *The Mythopoeic Reality: The Postwar American Nonfiction Novel* (Urbana: University of Illinois Press, 1976); Patrick Brantlinger, *The Reading Lesson: The Threat of Mass Literacy in Nineteenth-Century British Fiction* (Bloomington: Indiana University Press, 1998), 5; Lennard J. Davis, *Factual Fictions: The Origins of the English Novel* (Philadelphia: University of Pennsylvania Press, 1997); Davis, *Factual Fictions*, 70; McKeon, *The Origins of the English Novel, 1600–1740*, 413; Watt, *The Rise of the Novel*, 32; Romberg, *Studies in the Narrative Technique of the First-Person Novel*, 68; Robert E. Scholes, James Phelan, and Robert Leland Kellogg, *The Nature of Narrative*, revised ed. (New York: Oxford University Press, 2006), 267.

35 Troy J. Bassett, "Genre: Documentary Novels," *At the Circulating Library: A Database of Victorian Fiction, 1837–1901*. www.victorianresearch.org/atcl/show_genre.php?gid=63 (accessed June 28, 2023).

36 Barbara Foley, *Telling the Truth: The Theory and Practice of Documentary Fiction* (New York: Cornell University Press, 1986), 25.

37 See Laura Rotunno, *Postal Plots in British Fiction, 1840–1898: Readdressing Correspondence in Victorian Culture* (Basingstoke: Palgrave Macmillan, 2013); Catherine J. Golden, *Posting It: The Victorian Revolution in Letter Writing* (Gainesville: University Press of Florida, 2010); Katie-Louise Thomas, *Postal Pleasures: Sex, Scandal, and Victorian Letters* (New York: Oxford University Press, 2012).

38 Charles Dickens, *Great Expectations* (London: Penguin), 3.

39 Dickens, *Great Expectations*, 3.

40 Avrom Fleishman, *The English Historical Novel: Walter Scott to Virginia Woolf* (Baltimore, MD: Johns Hopkins University Press, 1971), 3.

41 Fleishman, *English Historical Novel*, 3–4.

42 Peter Brooks, *Realist Vision* (New Haven, CT: Yale University Press, 2008), 5.

43 Caroline Levine, *Forms: Whole, Rhythm, Hierarchy, Network* (Princeton, NJ: Princeton University Press, 2015), 3, 4.

44 Caroline Levine, "Not Against Structure, but in Search of Better Structures: A Response to Winfried Fluck," *American Literary History* 31 no. 2 (2019): 257.

45 Levine, *Forms*, 10–11.

46 David Herman, James Phelan, Peter J. Rabinowitz, Brian Richardson, and Robyn Warhol, *Narrative Theory: Core Concepts and Critical Debates* (Columbus: Ohio State University Press, 2012), 13.

47 Monika Gehlawat, "Myth and Mimetic Failure in 'The Remains of the Day,'" *Contemporary Literature* 54, no. 3 (2013): 491.

48 Mikhail Bakhtin, "Epic and Novel: Towards a Methodology for the Study of the Novel," in *The Dialogic Imagination*, ed. Michael Holquist (Austin: University of Texas Press), 45.

Chapter One: Epistolary Novels

1 For information on the numbers of epistolary novels published at the turn of the nineteenth century, charting the form's decline in popularity, see Frank Gees Black, *The Epistolary Novels in the Late Eighteenth Century: A Descriptive and Bibliographical Study* (Eugene: University of Oregon, 1940), 160–68. Black counts 160 published in the 1780s, 155 in the 1790s, 38 in the 1810s, and 26 in the 1820s. For a fuller listing of epistolary novels published in the nineteenth century and a description of the limitations of Black's list, see Kathleen Martha Ward, "Dear Sir or Madam: The Epistolary Novel in Britain in the Nineteenth Century," PhD thesis, University of Wisconsin, 1989.

2 English Showalter, *The Evolution of the French Novel: 1641–1782* (Princeton, NJ: Princeton University Press, 1972), 121.

3 Siv Gøril Brandtzæg, "The Epistolary Novel, An Annotated Bibliography," Oxford Bibliographies, British and Irish Literature" (2013). DOI: 10.1093/OBO/9780199846719-0079. See also Thomas O. Beebee, *Epistolary Fiction in Europe, 1500–1850* (Cambridge: Cambridge University Press, 1999) and Ian Watt, *The Rise of the Novel: Studies in Defoe, Richardson, and Fielding* (Berkeley: University of California Press, 1957).

4 Ward, "Dear Sir or Madam," 3.

5 For further discussion of free indirect discourse as "the largely successful solution to the problems of interpretation, authority, and believability" of epistolary novels, see the introductory chapter to Watt, *The Rise of the Novel*, and Elaine McGirr, "Interiorities," in *The Cambridge History of the English Novel*, ed. Robert Caserio and Clement Hawes (Cambridge: Cambridge University Press, 2012), 93.

6   George Levine, *How to Read the Victorian Novel* (Oxford: Wiley-Black-well, 2007), 32. Levine goes on to say later in his book that "Free indirect discourse is a remarkably devious invention in that it is extremely good at creating the illusion that consciousness is being rendered without authorial intervention, and that the language is the strictest representation … of the workings of a real character's mind" (63). His emphasis that free indirect discourse is still an illusory tactic calls to mind Carlyle's words opening this book arguing that fiction writers lie "more than we suspect."

7   William M. Sale, Jr., "Introduction," in Samuel Richardson, *Pamela*, ed. William M. Sale, Jr. (New York: Norton, 1958), v-xiv. Sale describes letter-writers as "popular since the reign of Elizabeth, when the rising middle class first provided a market for books of instruction. Among those whose culture is not commensurate with their new-found prosperity, education of one sort or another is always in demand, and letter-writers had continued for two hundred years to supply a felt need" (v). For other examples of letter-writing manuals, see *The New Lover's Instructor; Or, Whole Art of Courtship* (1780), Samuel Richardson's *Letters Written to and for Particular Friends* (1741), and Lewis Carroll's *Eight or Nine Wise Words about Letter-Writing* (1890). For scholarship on letter-writing manuals and their impact on fiction featuring letters, see Laura Rotunno, *Postal Plots in British Fiction, 1840–1898: Readdressing Correspondence in Victorian Culture* (Basingstoke: Palgrave Macmillan, 2013), chapters 1 and 2.

8   Thomas Cooke, *The Universal Letter-Writer; Or, New Art of Polite Correspondence* (London: Printed for J. Cooke, 1775), ix. The full title of Cooke's book illustrates the practicality of such a publication and its pedagogical value: *The Universal Letter-Writer; Or, New Art of Polite Correspondence; Containing a Course of Interesting Original Letters on the Most Important, Instructive, and Entertaining Subjects, Which May Serve as Copies for Inditing Letters on the various Occurrences in Life … To Which is Added The Complete Petitioner … Also, A new plain and easy Grammar of the English Language, and Directions for addressing Persons of all Ranks, either in Writing or Discourse. Likewise, Forms of Mortgages, Letters of Licence, Bonds, Indentures, Wills, Wills and Powers, Letter of Attorney, &c. &c. &c.*

9   Cooke, *Universal Letter-Writer*, x.

10   While I focus on epistolary novels here—novels narrated entirely through letters—many more Victorian novels feature letters as a source of "plot movement, characterization, and the 'reality effect.'" Rotunno, *Postal Plots*, unpag. A letter containing news of a dramatic event can propel a plot forward, a letter revealing a character's never-before-professed romantic attachment can reveal true intentions, and a letter delivering information about a business interest can remind readers that these characters reside in a realistic world. For more analysis on the letter's vital

place in British novels, see Rotunno, *Postal Plots* and Eve Tavor Bannet, *The Letters in the Story: Narrative-Epistolary Fiction from Aphra Behn to the Victorians* (Cambridge: Cambridge University Press, 2021). For more information on the Victorians and letter writing, see Catherine J. Golden, *Posting It: The Victorian Revolution in Letter Writing* (Gainesville: University Press of Florida, 2010).

11   Research published by the Smithsonian's National Postal Museum suggests a resurgence of epistolary novels in the twenty-first century, with novels including letters as well as more modern communication technologies like emails and text messages as narrative vehicles. See "Number of Epistolary Novels over Time," Smithsonian National Postal Museum (undated). https://postalmuseum.si.edu/research-articles/epistolary-fiction-development-of-the-epistolary-novel/number-of-epistolary-novels (accessed July 1, 2023).

12   Caroline Levine, *Forms: Whole, Rhythm, Hierarchy, Network* (Princeton, NJ: Princeton University Press, 2015), 6.

13   Anne Brontë, *The Tenant of Wildfell Hall*, ed. Stevie Davies (London: Penguin, 2016), 9.

14   Brontë, *Tenant of Wildfell Hall*, 9.

15   Brontë, *Tenant of Wildfell Hall*, 10.

16   Brontë, *Tenant of Wildfell Hall*, 10.

17   Brontë, *Tenant of Wildfell Hall*, 21.

18   Jan B. Gordon, "Gossip, Diary, Letter, Text: Anne Brontë's Narrative *Tenant* and the Problematic of the Gothic Sequel," *ELH* 51, no. 4 (1984): 719.

19   An edition of Acton Bell's novel published in 1854 removed the introductory framing letter to Halford altogether and instead started with Chapter 1's opening sentence, "You must go back with me to the autumn of 1827." Stevie Davis, the editor of the Penguin *Tenant of Wildfell Hall*, describes this "cheap edition … priced one shilling and sixpence" as a "corrupt text, which is highly expurgated" and "worthless to the modern editor" (492). See a digitized version of the 1854 book at https://archive.org/details/in.ernet.dli.2015.546508 (accessed July 1, 2023).

20   Ward, "Dear Sir or Madam," 153.

21   Hayley Horvath, "Laurence Housman Publishes An Englishwoman's Love-Letters," Cove Editions (undated). https://editions.covecollective.org/chronologies/laurence-housman-publishes-englishwomans-love-letters (accessed July 1, 2023).

22   In his piece for the *New Yorker*, Waldman puts *Clarissa*'s extraordinary length of "some nine hundred and seventy thousand words" into context: "For reference, 'War and Peace' clocks in a five hundred and sixty thousand words, and 'Infinite Jest' a slender four hundred and eighty-four thousand."

23   Elizabeth Hollis Berry, *Anne Brontë's Radical Vision: Structures of Consciousness*, English Literary Studies Monograph Series (Oak Bay, BC: University of Victoria, 1994), 62.

24   Deborah Denenholz Morse, "'I Speak of Those I Do Know': Witnessing as Radical Gesture in *The Tenant of Wildfell Hall*," in *New Approaches to the Literary Art of Anne Brontë*, ed. Julie Nash and Barbara A. Suess (Aldershot: Ashgate Publishing, 2001), 104.

25   Elizabeth Leaver, "Why Anne Brontë Wrote as She Did," *Brontë Studies* 32, no. 3 (2007): 240.

26   Brontë, *Tenant of Wildfell Hall*, 3.

27   Present-day experts in domestic violence frequently use something called "The Duluth Model" to help advocates understand what domestic abuse looks like and to help victims recognize the ways in which they were abused. This model emphasizes that domestic violence involves a wide range of behaviors that reinforce each other and contribute to an abuser's ability to have and keep power over his victim. One remarkable thing about Brontë's novel is not only the detail with which she paints Arthur's dissipation and Helen's psychological turmoil, but also how well her depiction of this marriage holds up to modern understandings of domestic abuse. "The Duluth Model" identifies eight "tactics" abusers use to maintain dominance over their partners: "using economic abuse," "using coercion and threats," "using intimidation," "using emotional abuse," "using isolation," "minimizing, denying, and blaming," "using children," and "using male privilege." For more detailed descriptions of these tactics and to see how they correspond with Arthur's manipulative behavior in *Tenant of Wildfell Hall*, see the "Power and Control Wheel," created by Domestic Abuse Intervention Programs. www.theduluthmodel.org/wp-content/uploads/2017/03/PowerandControl.pdf (accessed July 1, 2023).

28   Brontë, *Tenant of Wildfell Hall*, 220.

29   Brontë, *Tenant of Wildfell Hall*, 355.

30   Brontë, *Tenant of Wildfell Hall*, 277.

31   Brontë, *Tenant of Wildfell Hall*, 278.

32   Brontë, *Tenant of Wildfell Hall*, 279.

33   Brontë, *Tenant of Wildfell Hall*, 357.

34   Brontë, *Tenant of Wildfell Hall*, 358.

35   Brontë, *Tenant of Wildfell Hall*, 4.

36   Brontë, *Tenant of Wildfell Hall*, 396.

37   Brontë, *Tenant of Wildfell Hall*, 33–34.

38   N. M. Jacobs, "Gender and Layered Narrative in 'Wuthering Heights' and 'The Tenant of Wildfell Hall,'" *Journal of Narrative Technique* 16, no. 3 (1986): 208.

39   Jacobs, "Gender and Layered Narrative," 204.

40 Senf makes a wonderful comparison between the Gilbert frame of *Tenant of Wildfell Hall* and the ending of Margaret Atwood's *A Handmaid's Tale* in which Offred's narrative ends and then is replaced with commentary from a Cambridge professor. As Senf notes, the professor "obviously misunderstands so much of what Offred's narrative has revealed about the relationship between men and women." He makes insensitive remarks and uses sexist language all while presenting Offred's incredible narrative to a room of fellow academics. Senf writes, "Certainly Helen's silence is in some ways as troubling to twentieth-century readers as Offred's, though Gilbert is much kinder and more thoughtful about his superior position than [Professor] Pieixoto" (449). See Carol A. Senf, *"The Tenant of Wildfell Hall*: Narrative Silences and Questions of Gender," *College English* 52, no. 4 (1990): 446–56.

41 Brontë, *Tenant of Wildfell Hall*, 3.

42 Brontë, *Tenant of Wildfell Hall*, 4.

43 "From an Unsigned Review, *Sharpe's London Magazine*, August 1848, vii, 181–4," in *The Brontës: The Critical Heritage*, ed. Miriam Allott (London: Routledge, 1974), 263.

44 See *Oxford English Dictionary* online, s.v. coarse, *adj.* 5b.

45 *Selected Letters of Charlotte Brontë*, ed. Margaret Smith (Oxford: Oxford University Press, 2007), 176.

46 "From an Unsigned Review, *Sharpe's London Magazine*," 265.

47 "Charles Kingsley, from an Unsigned Review, *Fraser's Magazine*, April 1849, xxxix, 417–32," in *The Brontës: The Critical Heritage*, 271.

48 Senf, *"The Tenant of Wildfell Hall*: Narrative Silences and Questions of Gender," 455.

49 Brontë, *Tenant of Wildfell Hall*, 128.

50 Brontë, *Tenant of Wildfell Hall*, 129.

51 Brontë, *Tenant of Wildfell Hall*, 10.

52 The book sold out of its first printing quite quickly. Laurence Housman describes the unexpected and profitable success of the novel in his autobiography, *The Unexpected Years*, writing that "When the book had been published about a week—expecting nothing, but wishing to see if it was being properly announced—I turned one day to the advertisement columns of *The Times*, and there read Mr. John Murray's apologies to his readers for the book having sold out: a new issue was in the press, and would be ready immediately." Laurence Housman, *The Unexpected Years* (London: Jonathan Cape, 1937), 164. The first edition was published in November of 1900 with another four impressions published over the next two months.

53 Laurence Housman, *An Englishwoman's Love-Letters* (London: John Murray, 1900), 23, 62, 138. https://archive.org/details/englishwoman-slov00housrich/page/n5/ (accessed July 1, 2023).

54   David Lodge, *The Art of Fiction: Illustrated from Classic and Modern Texts* (New York: Viking, 1992), 24.

55   Housman, *Unexpected Years*, 164.

56   Housman, *An Englishwoman's Love-Letters*, 1.

57   Housman, *An Englishwoman's Love-Letters*, 1–2.

58   Housman, *An Englishwoman's Love-Letters*, 2.

59   Housman, *Unexpected Years*, 164.

60   William Zachs, Peter Isaac, Angus Fraser, and William Lister, "Murray family (per. 1768–1967), publishers," *Oxford Dictionary of National Biography* online (2004). https://doi.org/10.1093/ref:odnb/64907 (accessed July 1, 2023).

61   Housman, *Unexpected Years*, 164–65.

62   Housman, *An Englishwoman's Love-Letters*, 242.

63   "The Tyranny of Love," *The Academy: A Weekly Review of Literature and Life* (December 1, 1900), 510.

64   "The Tyranny of Love," 511.

65   Housman, *An Englishwoman's Love-Letters*, 5, 19, 26.

66   "The Tyranny of Love," 511.

67   Housman, *Unexpected Years*, 173.

68   "Letters of the Brownings," *Saturday Review of Politics, Literature, Science and Art* (February 25, 1899), 243.

69   "The Letters of Robert Browning and Elizabeth Barrett Barrett, 1845–6," *The Athenæum*, no. 3721 (February 18, 1899): 201.

70   "The Letters of Robert Browning and Elizabeth Barrett Barrett, 1845–6," 201.

71   "Letters of the Brownings," 243.

72   "Discretion and Publicity: Art. VI," *Edinburgh Review* 189, no. 388 (April 1899): 420.

73   "Discretion and Publicity," 426.

74   "Discretion and Publicity," 432, 428, 439.

75   Another period of public debate regarding the publication of love letters occurred following the publication of *Letters of John Keats to Fanny Brawne* in 1878. In fact, some reviews of the Browning collection compare and contrast it to Keats's letters and their controversial publication.

76   "Phi," "Correspondence: 'An Englishwoman's Love-Letters,'" *The Academy* 1493 (December 15, 1900): 610. *The Letters of Elizabeth Barrett Browning* were edited by Frederic G. Kenyon and published in London in 2 volumes by Smith, Elder, & Co. in 1897.

77   Housman, *Unexpected Years*, 119.

78   See *Another Englishwoman's Love-Letters* by Barry Pain (London: T. Fisher Unwin, 1901) and *The Lover's Replies to an Englishwoman's Love-Letters* (New York: Dodd, Mead, 1901).

Chapter Two: Life-Writing Novels

1   See the next chapter for a more detailed description of other characteristics that life-writing and adventure novels share.

2   Bram Stoker, *Dracula*, 351.

3   Chris Baldick, *The Oxford Dictionary of Literary Terms* (New York: Oxford University Press, 2008), s.v. "autobiography."

4   Baldick, *Oxford Dictionary of Literary Terms*, s.v. "memoir."

5   Heidi L. Pennington, *Creating Identity in the Victorian Fictional Autobiography* (Columbia: University of Missouri Press, 2018), 19.

6   Pennington, *Creating Identity*, 37.

7   Pennington, *Creating Identity*, 25.

8   See pp. 24–26 of the introduction to Pennington's *Creating Identity* for further discussion on how she differentiates between fictional autobiographies and non-autobiographical first-person novels like Robert Louis Stevenson's *Kidnapped*, F. Scott Fitzgerald's *The Great Gatsby*, and Herman Melville's *Moby Dick*.

9   Because Pennington's book so thoroughly covers *Jane Eyre* and *David Copperfield*, I only talk about them generally here. I highly recommend her book to those who want more in-depth analysis of the two novels.

10   Pennington, *Creating Identity*, 5.

11   Desirée Henderson's *Diary Index* (diaryindex.com) houses helpful lists of diary fiction and digitized diaries from the eighteenth to the twenty-first centuries.

12   Desirée Henderson, *How to Read a Diary: Critical Contexts and Interpretive Strategies for 21st-Century Readers* (London: Routledge, 2019), 5.

13   Henderson, *How to Read a Diary*, 2, 3.

14   Catherine Delafield, *Women's Diaries as Narrative in the Nineteenth-Century Novel* (London: Routledge, 2017), 15.

15   Henderson, *How to Read a Diary*, 76.

16   Trevor Field, *Form and Function in the Diary Novel* (Basingstoke: Palgrave Macmillan, 2014), 7.

17   Henderson, *How to Read a Diary*, 115.

18   I discuss the widespread use of this kind of posturing in non-fiction and fiction travel writing in Chapter 3, but these kinds of statements are also regularly present in epistolary and casebook novels (see Chapters 1 and 4 respectively).

19   Anne Brontë, *Agnes Grey* (Oxford: Oxford University Press, 2010), 5.

20   Brontë, *Agnes Grey*, 33.

21   Brontë, *Agnes Grey*, 54.

22   Brontë, *Agnes Grey*, 98.

23   Pennington, *Creating Identity*, 51.

24   Brontë, *Agnes Grey*, 173.

25 Garrett Stewart, "Narrative Economies in *The Tenant of Wildfell Hall*," in *New Approaches to the Literary Art of Anne Brontë*, ed. Julie Nash and Barbara A. Suess (Aldershot: Ashgate Publishing, 2001), 84.

26 "Introduction," Thomas Carlyle, *Sartor Resartus*, ed. Kerry McSweeney and Peter Sabor (Oxford: Oxford University Press, 2008), vii.

27 Vanessa L. Ryan, "The Unreliable Editor: Carlyle's *Sartor Resartus* and the Art of Biography," *Review of English Studies* NS 54, no. 215 (2003): 287.

28 J. Hillis Miller, *Victorian Subjects* (Durham, NC: Duke University Press, 1990), 305. George Levine discusses Carlyle's use of fictional elements but argues against considering the book a novel in "*Sartor Resartus* and the Balance of Fiction," *Victorian Studies* 8, no. 2 (1964): 131–60.

29 Carlyle, *Sartor Resartus*, 6.

30 *Sartor Resartus* was first published anonymously in monthly issues in *Fraser's Magazine* over several months in 1833 and 1834. In 1836, it was published in book form in the United States and included a preface written by Ralph Waldo Emerson. Carlyle added the subtitle, "The Life and Opinions of Herr Teufelsdröckh" to the edition published in England in 1838.

31 Carlyle, *Sartor Resartus*, 8.

32 Ryan, "The Unreliable Editor," 299.

33 Carlyle, *Sartor Resartus*, 8.

34 Carlyle, *Sartor Resartus*, 10.

35 Carlyle, *Sartor Resartus*, 58.

36 Carlyle, *Sartor Resartus*, 60.

37 Henderson, *How to Read a Diary*, 125.

38 Carlyle, *Sartor Resartus*, 60.

39 Carlyle, *Sartor Resartus*, 60–61.

40 Carlyle, *Sartor Resartus*, 112.

41 Carlyle, *Sartor Resartus*, 84.

42 Carlyle, *Sartor Resartus*, 118–19.

43 Carlyle, *Sartor Resartus*, 152–53.

44 Carlyle, *Sartor Resartus*, 221.

45 Ryan, "The Unreliable Editor," 290.

46 Miller, *Victorian Subjects*, 304.

47 Miller, *Victorian Subjects*, 307.

48 Miller, *Victorian Subjects*, 318.

49 Pennington, *Creating Identity*, 19.

50 Pennington, *Creating Identity*, 68.

51 Pennington, *Creating Identity*, "Introduction."

52 Linda H. Peterson, *Traditions of Victorian Women's Autobiography: The Poetics and Politics of Life Writing* (Charlottesville: University Press of Virginia, 1999), 264. See also Linda H. Peterson, *Victorian Autobiography:*

The Tradition of Self-Interpretation (New Haven, CT: Yale University Press, 1986).

53 Peterson, *Traditions of Victorian Women's Autobiography*, 263.

54 Anna Gibson, "Charlotte Brontë's First Person," *Narrative* 25, no. 2 (2017): 204.

55 Peterson, *Traditions of Victorian Women's Autobiography*, 244.

56 Carlyle, *Sartor Resartus*, 154.

57 Carlyle, *Sartor Resartus*, 27.

58 Carlyle, *Sartor Resartus*, 204.

59 Charlotte Brontë, *Jane Eyre* (Oxford: Oxford University Press, 2008), 448.

60 Thackeray's novel was published serially in *Fraser's Magazine* throughout 1844 under the title *"The Luck of Barry Lyndon: A Romance of the Last Century* by Fitz-Boodle," who identifies himself in the text through editorial footnotes and occasional bits of commentary and fact-checking. Thackeray later made significant revisions to the text when preparing it for inclusion in *Miscellanies: Prose and Verse* (1856), including limiting the presence of the novel's supposed "editor," Fitz-Boodle.

61 Although Redmond Barry was not a real person, Thackeray did borrow elements of his life story from historical persons. See Sanders's "Introduction" for further discussion of influences, particularly that of Andrew Robinson Bowes. William Makepeace Thackeray, *Barry Lyndon*, ed. Andrew Sanders (Oxford: Oxford World's Classics, 1999).

62 Anthony Trollope, *Thackeray*, ed. Richard Pearson (London: Routledge, 2016), 75.

63 Sanders, "Introduction," Thackeray, *Barry Lyndon*, xiii.

64 Thackeray, *Barry Lyndon*, 3.

65 Thackeray, *Barry Lyndon*, 38.

66 Thackeray, *Barry Lyndon*, 109.

67 Thackeray, *Barry Lyndon*, 113.

68 Thackeray, *Barry Lyndon*, 111–12.

69 Robert P. Fletcher, "'Proving a Thing Even While You Contradict It': Fictions, Beliefs, and Legitimation in 'The Memoirs of Barry Lyndon, Esq.'" *Studies in the Novel* 27, no. 4 (1995): 497.

70 Thackeray, *Barry Lyndon*, 134.

71 Thackeray, *Barry Lyndon*, 14.

72 Thackeray, *Barry Lyndon*, 128.

73 "Barry Lyndon," *Saturday Review* (December 1856): 784.

74 Fletcher, "'Proving a Thing Even While You Contradict It,'" 504.

75 Elizabeth Bleicher, "Legible Liars: Thackeray's *Barry Lyndon* as Professor of Imposture," *Pivot: A Journal of Interdisciplinary Studies and Thought* 1 (2011): 36. https://pivot.journals.yorku.ca/index.php/pivot/article/view/32155/29374 (accessed July 1, 2023).

76 Bleicher, "Legible Liars," 35.

77 Thackeray, *Barry Lyndon*, 126–27.
78 Robert A. Colby, "Barry Lyndon and the Irish Hero," *Nineteenth-Century Fiction*
21, no. 2 (1966): 112.
79 Thackeray, *Barry Lyndon*, 307, 309.
80 Carlyle, *Sartor Resartus*, 225.

Chapter Three: Travel and Adventure Novels

1   Caroline Levine, *Forms: Whole, Rhythm, Hierarchy, Network* (Princeton, NJ: Princeton University Press, 2015), 9.
2   Pat Barr, *A Curious Life for a Lady: The Story of Isabella Bird* (London: John Murray, 1970), 173.
3   Barr, *Curious Life for a Lady*, 19.
4   Barr, *Curious Life for a Lady*, 341.
5   Many of these editions can be viewed in full on Archive.org through digitized collections from Brigham Young University, the University of Toronto, the Public Library of India, the Majority World Collection, and the California Digital Library. In her biography, *The Life of Isabella Bird* (London: John Murray, 1906), Anna M. Stoddart also regularly notes Bird's additional work on subsequent editions of her writing.
6   Barr, *Curious Life for a Lady*, 197.
7   Dorothy Middleton, "Bishop [née Bird], Isabella Lucy (1831–1904), traveller," *Oxford Dictionary of National Biography* online (2004). https://doi.org/10.1093/ref:odnb/31904 (accessed July 1, 2023).
8   "Rocky Mountain Romance," review of the first edition of *A Lady's Life in the Rocky Mountains, Spectator* (November 8, 1897): 1414.
9   Isabella Lucy Bird, *A Lady's Life in the Rocky Mountains* (New York: G. P. Putnam's Sons, 1879), 123.
10 "Books of Travel," *The Examiner* (January 3, 1880): 22.
11 "Books of Travel," 22.
12 The University of California Libraries' copy of Whymper's book, including the illustrations and maps mentioned, has been digitized and can be viewed in its entirety at archive.org/details/ascentofmatterho00whym/ (accessed July 1, 2023).
13 "Books of Travel," 22.
14 "Books of Travel," 22.
15 "Rocky Mountain Romance," 1414.
16 Carl Thompson, *Travel Writing* (Abingdon: Routledge, 2011), 27–28.
17 Susan Bassnett, "Travel Writing and Gender," in Peter Hulme and Tim Youngs, eds., *The Cambridge Companion to Travel Writing* (Cambridge: Cambridge University Press, 2002), 235.

18 Robert Louis Stevenson, "A Humble Remonstrance," *Longman's Magazine* 5 (December 1884): 141.

19 Isabella Lucy Bird, *The Hawaiian Archipelago: Six Months among the Palm Groves, Coral Reefs, and Volcanoes of the Sandwich Islands* (London: John Murray, 1906), x.

20 Bird, *Hawaiian Archipelago*, ix–x.

21 Bird, *A Lady's Life in the Rocky Mountains*.

22 Barr, *Curious Life for a Lady*, 20. Christine DeVine goes into more detail about what that editing process looked like in the case of Bird's Colorado book. See Christine DeVine, "Isabella Bird and Mountain Jim: Geography and Gender Boundaries in *A Lady's Life in the Rocky Mountains*," *Nineteenth-Century Gender Studies* 3, no. 2 (2007).

23 Mary Seacole, *Wonderful Adventures of Mrs. Seacole in Many Lands*, ed. W. J. S. (London: James Blackwood, 1857), 1–2.

24 Evelyn J. Hawthorne discusses the similarity of Seacole's opening sentence to those of nineteenth-century slave narratives. See "Self-Writing, Literary Traditions, and Post-Emancipation Identity: The Case of Mary Seacole," *Biography* 23, no. 2 (2000): 309–31.

25 Angelica Poon, "Comic Acts of (Be)longing: Performing Englishness in Wonderful Adventures of Mrs. Seacole in Many Lands," *Victorian Literature and Culture* 35 (2007): 505.

26 Alisha R. Walters convincingly argues that Seacole also "positions her 'Creole' body, which she codes as being emotionally responsive, as one that is both unfamiliar, but in many ways *superior*, to those of her comparatively emotionally repressed British readers." See Alisha R. Walters, "'The tears I could not repress, rolling down my brown cheeks': Mary Seacole, Feeling, and the Imperial Body," *Nineteenth-Century Gender Studies* 16, no. 1 (2020): 41–58.

27 Number found through the author's search of the WorldCat library catalog (www.worldcat.org/).

28 Felix Driver, "Stanley, Sir Henry Morton (1841–1904), explorer and journalist," *Oxford Dictionary of National Biography* online (2004). https://doi.org/10.1093/ref:odnb/36247 (accessed July 1, 2023).

29 Henry M. Stanley, *How I Found Livingstone: Travels, Adventures, and Discoveries in Central Africa; Including Four Months' Residence with Dr. Livingstone* (London: Sampson Low, Marston, Low, and Searle, 1872), xv.

30 Stanley, *How I Found Livingstone*, xvii.

31 Mary H. Kingsley, *Travels in West Africa: Congo Français, Corisco and Cameroons* (London: Macmillan, 1897), vii.

32 Kingsley, *Travels in West Africa*, viii.

33 "Rocky Mountain Romance," 1414.

34 "Books of Travel," 22.

35   H. Rider Haggard, *She: A History of Adventure* (London: Longman, Green, & Co., 1887).

36   H. Rider Haggard, *King Solomon's Mines* (London: Cassell & Company, 1885), 27.

37   Ken Gelder, *Popular Fiction: The Logics and Practices of a Literary Field* (Abingdon: Routledge, 2004), 42.

38   Robert Louis Stevenson, "My First Book: 'Treasure Island,'" *Idler* (August 1894), reprinted in Stevenson, *Treasure Island*, ed. John Seelye (Harmondsworth: Penguin Books, 1999).

39   For a discussion of American literature's influence on *Treasure Island*, see John Seelye's introduction to the Penguin edition.

40   Robert Louis Stevenson, *An Inland Voyage* (London: C. Kegan Paul & Co., 1878), v.

41   Stevenson, *An Inland Voyage*, v–vi.

42   Stevenson, *An Inland Voyage*, vi.

43   Robert Louis Stevenson, *Travels with a Donkey in the Cévennes* (Boston: Roberts Brothers, 1879), 5.

44   For an in-depth description of Stevenson's changes to the serialized version of *Treasure Island*, see David Angus, "Youth on the Prow: The First Publication of Treasure Island," *Studies in Scottish Literature* 25, no. 1 (1990): 83–99.

45   Robert Louis Stevenson, *Treasure Island* (London: Cassell & Company, 1883), vi.

46   R. M. Ballantyne, *The Coral Island: A Tale of the Pacific Ocean* (London: T. Nelson & Sons, 1857), i.

47   For further discussion of the origins and creation of this map, see John Sutherland's introduction to the Broadview edition of *Treasure Island* as well as Sally Bushell, "Mapping Victorian Adventure Fiction: Silences, Doublings, and the Ur-Map in *Treasure Island* and *King Solomon's Mines*," *Victorian Studies* 57, no. 4 (2015): 611–37.

48   Bushell, "Mapping Victorian Adventure Fiction," 625. One can view the original full-color version of this map in the first edition of *Treasure Island* published by Cassell & Company in 1883 in the California Digital Library collection on Archive.org. https://archive.org/details/islandtreasure00stevrich/page/n7/ (accessed July 1, 2023).

49   Sally Bushell, "Paratext or Imagetext? Interpreting the Fictional Map," *Word & Image: A Journal of Verbal/Visual Enquiry* 32, no. 2 (2016): 183.

50   Stevenson, *Treasure Island*, 283.

51   Bushell, "Mapping Victorian Adventure Fiction," 612.

52   The original serialization can be viewed online in the digital collections of the University of South Carolina Libraries. https://digital.library.sc.edu/collections/robert-louis-stevensons-kidnapped-in-young-folks-paper/

(accessed July 1, 2023). A first edition of the single volume, including the color fold-out map, can be viewed online in the National Library of Scotland's digital collection. https://digital.nls.uk/74554868 (accessed July 1, 2023).

53   Robert Louis Stevenson, *Kidnapped* (London: Cassell & Company, 1886), 107.   https://archive.org/details/kidnappedbeingm03stevgoog/page/n8/ (accessed July 1, 2023).

54   Stevenson, *Kidnapped*, 101.

55   Stevenson, *Kidnapped*, iii.

56   "Tom Sleigh Reads Seamus Heaney," *New Yorker* poetry podcast, May 20, 2017. www.wnyc.org/story/tom-sleigh-reads-seamus-heaney/ (accessed July 1, 2023).

57   Stevenson, *Treasure Island*, 1.

58   Stevenson, *Treasure Island*, 5–6.

59   Stevenson, *Treasure Island*, 216–17.

60   Stevenson, *Treasure Island*, 117.

61   Stevenson, *Treasure Island*, 118.

62   Stevenson, *Treasure Island*, 122.

63   Stevenson, *Treasure Island*, 123.

64   Stevenson, *Treasure Island*, 125.

65   Alexandra Valint, "The Child's Resistance to Adulthood in Robert Louis Stevenson's *Treasure Island*: Refusing to Parrot," *English Literature in Transition, 1880–1920* 58, no. 1 (2015): 4. Valint writes that many critics have ignored this narrative shift in the novel but provides a thorough rebuttal to those who have overlooked it.

66   Morton N. Cohen, "Haggard, Sir (Henry) Rider (1856–1925), novelist," *Oxford Dictionary of National Biography* online (2004). https://doi.org/10.1093/ref:odnb/33632 (accessed July 1, 2023).

67   C. S. Lewis, "The Mythopoeic Gift of Rider Haggard," *On Stories and Other Essays on Literature*, ed. Walter Hooper (New York: Harcourt, 1982), 98.

68   Nathan Hensley, *Forms of Empire: The Poetics of Victorian Sovereignty* (Oxford: Oxford University Press, 2016), 195.

69   Andrew M. Stauffer, "Introduction," H. Rider Haggard, *She: A History of Adventure* (Peterborough: Broadview, 2006), 11.

70   Kate Holterhoff, "She, A History of Adventure," *Visual Haggard*. http://www.visualhaggard.org/novels/34 (accessed February 13, 2020).

71   Over two thousand illustrations from Haggard novels are viewable on VisualHaggard.org thanks to the diligent archiving of Kate Holterhoff.

72   Haggard, *She*, 32.

73   Haggard, *She*, 11.

74   Haggard, *She*, 12.

75   Haggard, *She*, 13.

76 For a discussion of Defoe's posturing in *Robinson Crusoe*, see the Intro-
    duction. For a discussion of Collins's *The Woman in White* and *The
    Moonstone* and their claims of authenticity, see the following chapter.

77 Haggard, *She*, 40.

78 Oscar Wilde, "The Decay of Lying—An Observation," in *The Collected
    Works of Oscar Wilde* (Hertfordshire: Wordsworth Editions, 1997), 924.

79 Wilde, "Decay of Lying," 929.

80 Wilde criticizes Stevenson's writing, too: "There is such a thing as robbing
    a story of its reality by trying to make it too true, and *The Black Arrow* is
    so inartistic as not to contain a single anachronism to boast of, while the
    transformation of Dr Jekyll reads dangerously like an experiment out of
    the *Lancet*" (924).

81 Patrick Brantlinger briefly notes some of the other parodies of Haggard's
    writing: "Andrew Lang penned a sonnet, "Twosh," dedicated to his friend
    "Hyder Ragged." He then coauthored, with W. H. Pollock, the tale of *He*,
    subtitled "by the authors of 'It,' 'King Solomon's Wives,' ... and other
    romances." And there were also George Forrest's "The Deathless Queen"
    and George Sims's "The Lost Author." See his entry on Haggard in *The
    Oxford Encyclopedia of British Literature*.

82 Charles Biron, *King Solomon's Wives, or, The Phantom Mines* (London:
    Vizetelly & Co., 1887), 9. https://babel.hathitrust.org/cgi/pt?id=uc1.
    b000716833 (accessed July 1, 2023).

83 Edward Said, *Culture and Imperialism* (New York: Alfred A. Knopf, 1993),
    62.

84 Said, *Culture and Imperialism*, 64.

85 Homi K. Bhabha, *The Location of Culture*, 2nd ed. (London: Rout-
    ledge, 1994), 122, 123.

86 Bhabha, *Location of Culture*, 126.

87 Rahul Rao, "Postcolonialism," in *The Oxford Handbook of Political
    Ideologies*, ed. Michael Freeden, Marc Stears, and Lyman Tower Sargent
    (Oxford: Oxford University Press, 2012).

88 Ronjaunee Chatterjee, Alicia Mireles Christoff, and Amy R. Wong,
    "Introduction: Undisciplining Victorian Studies," *Victorian Studies* 62,
    no. 3 (2020): 374.

89 Chatterjee, Christoff, and Wong, "Introduction: Undisciplining Victo-
    rian Studies," 375.

Chapter Four: Casebook Novels

1   Roger Luckhurst, "Introduction," Bram Stoker, *Dracula* (Oxford: Oxford
    World's Classics, 2011), xiv. Mary Shelley's *Frankenstein* is a good example
    of a gothic documentary novel. Criscillia Benford calls it a "multilevel
    structure." See "'Listen to my tale': Multilevel Structure, Narrative Sense

Making, and the Inassimilable in Mary Shelley's *Frankenstein*," *Narrative* 18, no. 3 (2010): 324–46.

2   A. B. Emrys, *Wilkie Collins, Vera Caspary and the Evolution of the Casebook Novel* (Jefferson, NC: McFarland & Co., 2011), 13.

3   Katrien Bollen and Raphaël Ingelbien, "An Intertext That Counts? *Dracula*, *The Woman in White*, and Victorian Imaginations of the Foreign Other," *English Studies* 90, no. 4 (2009): 405.

4   Elisha Cohn, "Suspending Detection: Collins, Dickens, and the Will to Know," *Dickens Studies Annual* 46 (2015): 268.

5   See *Oxford English Dictionary* online, s.v. casebook, *n.* 1.

6   Lauren Kassell, Michael Hawkins, Robert Ralley, and John Young, "History of Medical Records," *A Critical Introduction to the Casebooks of Simon Forman and Richard Napier, 1596–1634*. https://casebooks.lib.cam.ac.uk/astrological-medicine/history-of-medical-records (accessed July 1, 2023).

7   For further discussion of the characteristics and history of eyewitness narration going back to Defoe, Richardson, and others, see Robert E. Scholes, James Phelan, and Robert Leland Kellogg, *The Nature of Narrative*, revised ed. (New York: Oxford University Press, 2006), chapter 7.

8   Wilkie Collins, *The Woman in White*, ed John Sutherland (Oxford: Oxford World's Classics, 2011 [1860]), 414.

9   Troy J. Bassett lists *Strange Case of Dr. Jekyll and Mr. Hyde* (1885) by Robert Louis Stevenson as a Victorian documentary novel in his "Genre: Documentary Novels," *At the Circulating Library: A Database of Victorian Fiction, 1837–1901*. www.victorianresearch.org/atcl/show_genre.php?gid=63 (accessed June 28, 2023). While the title's inclusion of the words "*Strange Case*" seems to make it a fitting work for this chapter, I have not included it in my study because Stevenson's novella is not entirely written in documents, which is the primary parameter of this book. Even so, some of the elements of casebook writing I discuss here could certainly apply to the novella. Furthermore, Luckhurst notes that Stoker "admired" Stevenson's book, so there are undoubtedly reasons to consider them together. See Luckhurst, "Introduction," Stoker, *Dracula*, xiv.

10   Stoker, *Dracula*, 59.

11   Alexander Welsh, *Strong Representations: Narrative and Circumstantial Evidence in England* (Baltimore, MD: Johns Hopkins University Press, 1992), 7.

12   The complete run of *The Woman in White* in *All the Year Round* can be viewed via Archive.org thanks to the University of Buckingham Library and *Dickens Journals Online*. https://archive.org/details/djo (accessed July 1, 2023).

13   The diary entries included in the novel begin on November 8 and go to June 20. For information regarding date discrepancies between the serialization and later editions, some of which are significant, see the John Sutherland's "Explanatory Notes" and "Appendix C: The Chronology of *The Woman in White*," in the Oxford World's Classics edition of *The Woman in White*.

14   Collins, *The Woman in White*, 342–43.

15   Collins, *The Woman in White*, 343.

16   Stoker, *Dracula*, 210. Despite this key difference, Collins's novels still provide a sense of immediacy rather than aftermath by the fact that Collins uses documents likes letters, diary entries, and legal documents which bear the markings of having been composed in the midst of the action. Thus, while some documents included in these novels have a more distant, reflective stance (Mr. Betteredge going on about the ever-timely wisdom of *Robinson Crusoe* in *The Moonstone*, for instance), other documents like Marian's diary in *The Woman in White* or the journal of Ezra Jennings in *The Moonstone* keep readers immersed in the action and give them a sense of immediacy.

17   Stoker, *Dracula*, 72.

18   Stoker, *Dracula*, 127.

19   Stoker, *Dracula*, 165.

20   Stoker, *Dracula*, 166.

21   Stoker, *Dracula*, 208.

22   David Seed, "The Narrative Method of *Dracula*," *Nineteenth-Century Fiction* 40, no. 1 (1985): 68.

23   Caroline Levine, *Forms: Whole, Rhythm, Hierarchy, Network* (Princeton, NJ: Princeton University Press, 2015), 9.

24   Stoker, *Dracula*, 351.

25   Wilkie Collins, *The Moonstone*, ed. John Sutherland (Oxford: Oxford World's Classics, 1999), 190.

26   Collins, *The Moonstone*, 252.

27   Collins, *The Moonstone*, 315.

28   Lynn Pykett, *The Nineteenth-Century Sensation Novel*, 2nd ed. (Tavistock: Northcote House Publishers, 2011 [1994]), 58.

29   Stoker, *Dracula*, 127.

30   Collins, *The Woman in White*, 27.

31   Collins, *The Woman in White*, 164.

32   Collins, *The Moonstone*, 1.

33   Collins, *The Moonstone*, 5.

34   Collins, *The Moonstone*, 6.

35   Collins, *The Moonstone*, 6.

36   Collins, *The Moonstone*, 6.

37   Collins, *The Woman in White*, 83.

38   Collins, *The Woman in White*, 450.

39   Collins, *The Woman in White*, 453.

40   Charles Warren Adams [Charles Felix], *The Notting Hill Mystery* (London: British Library, 2015 [1862–63]), 1.

41   Adams, *Notting Hill Mystery*, 174.

42   Adams, *Notting Hill Mystery*, 5.

43   Adams, *Notting Hill Mystery*, 234–35.

44   Cheryl Blake Price, *Chemical Crimes: Science and Poison in Victorian Crime Fiction* (Columbus: Ohio State University Press, 2019), 116.

45   Stephen Knight, *Crime Fiction since 1800: Detection, Death, Diversity*, 2nd ed. (London: Red Globe Press, 2010 [2004]), 47.

46   Stoker, *Dracula*, 351.

47   Modern-day editions of Collins's novel do not include the "Preamble" label used in the original serialization. These editions use the "New Edition" of 1861 as their primary source, which erases the "Preamble" label and instead begins with "The Story begun by Walter Hartright, of Clement's Inn, Teacher of Drawing." The "Preamble" label is useful, though, because it appropriately distinguishes the first several paragraphs of the novel, which are written in the third person and provide a description of the casebook's contents, purpose, and method. In the novel's first serial installment, the section labeled "The Story Begun by Walter Hartright …" is written in the first person. Both, we are told, are written by Walter, but the third-person perspective of the "Preamble" section provides a sense of critical distance and objectivity, which the subsequent first-person narrative does not have. The two sections establish Walter as both outside, as official editor, and as central character.

48   Collins, *The Woman in White*, 5–6.

49   In his excellent essay, "The Sensationalism of *The Woman in White*," *Nineteenth-Century Fiction* 32, no. 1 (1977): 18–35, Walter M. Kendrick argues that once Laura is welcomed home again as her true self, and "all villainy" has been "disposed of, the pugnacious 'Preamble' has lost its motivation. The reason for the novel's existence, which it provides with great care on page one, has been used up by its end. In retrospect, it looks as if there never was any reason for the novel to exist at all" (32). "The technique of first-person testimony, which the 'Preamble' claims will make the events clear and positive, is the principal means by which they become blurred and ambiguous" (33).

50   Collins, *The Woman in White*, 450.

51   Collins, *The Woman in White*, 452.

52   Collins, *The Woman in White*, 454.

53   Kendrick, "Sensationalism," 31.

54   Collins, *The Woman in White*, 464.

55   Collins, *The Moonstone*, 7.

56 Collins, *The Moonstone*, 7.
57 Collins, *The Moonstone*, 7–8.
58 Collins, *The Moonstone*, 189–90.
59 Collins, *The Moonstone*, 238.
60 Collins, *The Moonstone*, 238.
61 Pykett, *Nineteenth-Century Sensation Novel*, 58.
62 Stoker, *Dracula*, 4.
63 Stoker, *Dracula*, 167.
64 Stoker, *Dracula*, 174.
65 Stoker, *Dracula*, 175.
66 Stoker, *Dracula*, 223.
67 Stoker, *Dracula*, 207.
68 Stephen Knight, *Form and Ideology in Crime Fiction*, new ed. (Basingstoke: Palgrave Macmillan, 1980), 8.
69 Maia McAleavey argues convincingly that Sir Walter Scott's novels also feature "the story of a group rather than an individual" and that this is a key affordance of the chronicle form. See her article for some of the ways that Scott's novels influenced Victorian historical and documentary fiction. Maia McAleavey, "Behind the Victorian Novel: Scott's *Chronicles*," *Victorian Studies* 61, no. 2 (2019): 232–39.

Conclusion

1 Dorrit Claire Cohn, *Transparent Minds: Narrative Modes for Presenting Consciousness in Fiction* (Princeton, NJ: Princeton University Press, 1984), 107.
2 The novel's chapter titles, indicating day, time, and location of each section's composition, traces this linear plotting from day one to day six.
3 Ishiguro, *The Remains of the Day* (London: Faber & Faber, 2011 [1989]), 74.
4 Ishiguro, *Remains of the Day*, 95.
5 Ishiguro, *Remains of the Day*, 109–10.
6 Ishiguro, *Remains of the Day*, 115.
7 Kathleen Wall, "*The Remains of the Day* and Its Challenges to Theories of Unreliable Narration," *Journal of Narrative Technique* 24, no. 1 (1994): 25.
8 Wall, "*The Remains of the Day* and Its Challenges," 23.
9 Ishiguro, *Remains of the Day*, 256.
10 Salman Rushdie, "Salman Rushdie: Rereading *The Remains of the Day* by Kazuo Ishiguro," *Guardian* (August 17, 2012).
11 As cited in part in my Introduction, Monika Gehlawat writes that

> Formalism is the key to *The Remains of the Day*, and for this reason, Ishiguro's project is inextricably bound up with that of his protagonist Mr. Stevens. In both novel and protagonist, the problem of

presentation and staging becomes the very texture of the emergent object as well as its central motivation for being. *The Remains of the Day* is constructed as a kind of Russian nesting doll of creative workmanship.

Monika Gehlawat, "Myth and Mimetic Failure in 'The Remains of the Day,'" *Contemporary Literature* 54, no. 3 (2013): 491.

12 Caroline Levine, "Not Against Structure, but in Search of Better Structures: A Response to Winfried Fluck," *American Literary History* 31 no. 2 (2019): 259.

13 Kazuo Ishiguro, *My Twentieth Century Evening and Other Small Breakthroughs* (London: Faber & Faber, 2017), 16.

Index